also by
PETRA WILLIAMS

Flow Blue China
An Aid to Identification
1971, Revised Edition, 1981

Flow Blue China II
1973, Revised Edition, 1981

Flow Blue China
and
Mulberry Ware
Similarity and Value Guide
1975, Revised Edition, 1981

Staffordshire
Romantic Transfer Patterns
Cup Plates and
Early Victorian China
1978

Staffordshire
II

Romantic Transfer Patterns

Cup Plates and
Early Victorian China

March 10th 1835

Thos. H. Dunn   Dpty Marshaw

1/2	dz	plain Tumblers	100	50
1/2	"	Cut do	300	1 50
1/2	"	plain Wines	150	75
1/2	"	Blue Plates		75
1/2	"	do Tureens		56
1/2	"	" Bowls	200	1 00
2		" do	75	1 50
4		Glass Plates 2/37 2/25		62
1	Sett	Blue Cups & Saucers		62
1	do	Lustre " "		87
1	Pair	Persian Ewer & Basons		75
1		Blue Teapot		75
1		" Sugar		50
1		" Cream		25
1		Pitcher		62
1	dz	Cup Plates 1/2 25 1/2 31		56
1		Blue dishes		1 00
2	Salt	Cellars		50
1/2	dz	Edg'd Tureens		31
2		Purple dishes 75 50		1 25
1/2	dz	" Plates		75

Importer's List of English dishes including cup plates. Rudd & Martin Day Book, Louisville, Kentucky, March 18th, 1830. Collection of the Filson Club, Louisville.

Petra Williams
Marguerite R. Weber

Staffordshire II

Romantic Transfer Patterns

*Cup Plates and
Early Victorian China*

FOUNTAIN HOUSE EAST
Jeffersontown, Kentucky

LIBRARY OF CONGRESS CATALOG CARD NUMBER 78-55047
ISBN 0-914736-09-4
SECOND PRINTING

ADDITIONAL COPIES OF THIS BOOK MAY
BE OBTAINED FROM

FOUNTAIN HOUSE EAST
P.O. BOX 99298
JEFFERSONTOWN, KENTUCKY 40299

Acknowledgements

The kind and knowledgeable people who corresponded with us and sent photographs and proofs of identification are presented here with much gratitude and affection. Their contributions widened the scope of our book. Their names are listed in alphabetical order. We sincerely regret if we have inadvertently omitted anyone.

Alma and Geoffrey Barnes, England; Clare Boyd and Colonel James Boyd, New Hampshire; Mr. and Mrs. Joseph Cline, Illinois; Chris Coleman, Maryland; Mary Copeland, Ontario; Sandra Correnty, Massachusetts; Howard Davis, England; Elaine De Carli, California; Katherine Dickson, Scotland; Pam and Paul Donath, Pennsylvania; Don Eator, Pennsylvania; Nancy Glendenning, Maine; Joan Gray, California; Rose Heironymus, Kentucky; Mrs. Thearon Hooks, North Carolina; Dr. and Mrs. Joseph Humphries, Massachusetts; Dr. Mina Johnson, North Carolina; Jean Kerr, Kentucky; Betty Keefer, Texas; Miriam Kimmel, New Jersey; Gloria Kleuver, North Carolina; William and Teresa Kurau, New York; Doris Lechler, Ohio; Pam Miller, New Jersey; Richard Moore, New York; Leonard Mosely, Florida; Terry McCandless, Tennessee; Henry McClure, Missouri; Jo McCullough, Alabama; Doris O'Leary, Illinois; Barbara Pond, Connecticut; Richard and Barbara Price, Pennsylvania; Mrs. E.J. Priestly, England; Clifton Sargent, Jr., Maine; Mary Sliker, N. Jersey Russell Schneider, New Hampshire; Cecilia Sternfield, New Jersey; Janice Stockman, Ohio; Paul Strouse, Ohio; Jane Swengel, Ohio; Arlene Thomas, Pennsylvania; Mark Thompson, California; Jean Todd, California; Selma Ullman, New Jersey; Stan Vanderlaan, New York; V. Stephen Vaughn, Massachusetts; J. Utley, England; Mrs. Harold Weeden, New Jersey; Priscilla Wegars, Idaho; Esther Wilson, California; Susan Williams, New York; Doris Willson, Kentucky.

Foreword

This book is presented as a sequel to our first treatise on Staffordshire china, "Staffordshire Romantic Transfer Patterns, Cup Plates and Early Victorian China" (1978.), which will hereinafter be referred to as Book I. Numerous patterns, different from those described in that book were discovered after 1978. Information poured in from collectors and dealers adding to the descriptions used in the first book, and many patterns listed as "unknown" as to maker or name were identified.

A revised edition of Book I was contemplated, but to add new material with the addenda and corrections would result in an immensely large, unwieldly and heavy book, costly to produce and thus necessitating a very high price. This book is being published as a separate volume, a supplement to Book I. Perhaps the studious reader will write in the corrections and additional information in his or her copy of the first book.

The first part of this second book is comprised of new material, and follows the format established in Book I. The middle section is devoted to transfer patterns in the form of pulls. The last section contains the corrections and addenda to the designs shown in Book I and is presented in the numerical order of the pages of that book.

Some correspondents, especially from England, asked why we did not specify colour with each picture. As was set out in the first book, transfer patterns were printed in many colours, but for the purpose of identification, which was our goal, colour is not important. The elements of the transfer border and of the parts of the central scenes take precedence when the dish bears no back-stamp or maker's mark and identification is essayed. An attempt is made in this new work to reply to the suggestions and requests that colour be noted. Bear in mind that pale blue is the most common, followed by "pink" (all red tones), sepia, black lavender, medium and dark blue (used mostly by early makers), green, and the rarest, yellow. Occasionally dishes are found with the border in one colour and the center scene in another, many are very attractive and are desirable acquisitions for display. I have been informed by a distinguished English authority that English collectors overwhelmingly prefer blue and white dishes. However "The World of Interiors" a beautiful and prestigious English shelter magazine devoted to the architectural and decorative arts carried a cover photograph on its March 1984 issue, showing a handsome mantel collection of pink, polychrome, lavender and light blue Staffordshire transfer-printed dishes. The large dark pink plate, at left in the arrangement is "William Penn's Treaty". The exact transfer appears on page 531 of our Book I.

Prices of Staffordshire china have advanced as dealers become more aware of the early dates that the dishes were potted, and of the identities and fame of many of the potters. As of this writing (July 1985) plates are $30.00-$50.00, platters $85.00-$125.00 and up (depending on size), handleless cups and saucers are about $50.00, and hollow ware (pots, sugar, creamers, gravy boats, sauce boats, etc.) are higher priced than plates, as are covered dishes and tureens as well as fancy dishes found in dessert services. Prices depend upon the condition of the item, the colour, size, the pattern and the potter. Cup plates are $50.00 - over $100.00 depending on all the above factors.

The size of the photographs in this book, as in Book I, are not in proportion to the dishes, as the pictures of the cup plates have been enlarged to show detail.

The Staffordshire collection of Fountain House East has been donated to the Margaret Woodbury Strong Museum at One Manhattan Square in Rochester, New York and will be on display there in the future.

We are grateful to our readers, visitors, and correspondents for their help, interest and encouragement. The compiling of the information for our book has not seemed like work, rather it has been an adventure in detection, a real pleasure to have had the opportunity to handle the colourful dishes and admire the ingenuity of the artists' pictures and border designs. The time granted to us was a blessing from the Lord, and we remain thankful to Him.

Petra Williams
Marguerite R. Weber

Jeffersontown, Kentucky
October 1985

Contents

11

Illustrations

Frontpiece. Importer's receipt list, Rudd & Martin Day Book. Louisville, Kentucky, March 18th, 1830.

PLATE I

Clews in Kentucky

Louisville, Kentucky
(from the Indiana shore)
12-1/2″ cobalt platter made by James and Ralph Clews.
Collection of William and Teresa Kurau

James Clews was born near Staffordshire, England, September 2, 1790 when his brother Ralph was two years old. By the time James was 25 we learn that he was in the pottery business. Jewitt *Ceramic Art in Great Britian* states that in 1818-19 the works of Andrew Stevenson were closed and "passed into the hands of Mr. James Clews." His brother had joined him and the company was known locally as J. & R. Clews. Their ususal mark was an impressed circle with double band containing the words Clews Warranted Staffordshire surrounding a large crown.**

According to an article by Frank Stefano, Jr. in Antiques magazine February 1974*, the brothers always rented their pottery works. At first they rented from William Adams for twenty five years, beginning in 1817 and later from Andrew Stevenson. Both potteries were in Cobridge and they are listed by Simon Shaw in 1829 *History of The Staffordshire Potteries* along with the great Samuel Alcock, and a few others as "making various kinds of Pottery and Porcelain . . . manufactured in great perfection."

The brothers captured a large American market for their wares. Their famous patterns made for America include the "States" with border showing the names of 15 states, the "Landing of Lafayette", The Picturesque Views" series showing the Hudson River scenes copied from the paintings of Wall.

The firm would seem to us successful with the American market known to have been immense, but the Clews were in financial trouble. They borrowed heavily from the estate of their deceased father. They were in debt to several potters also. Job Meigh forced them into bankruptcy in 1827 and they had to sell off most of their stock. They survived this difficulty and continued to make transfer ware. They also operated their father's brewery and opened other new businesses related to the pottery. However, in November 1834 they were declared bankrupt. When they failed William Adams one of the main creditors who had furnished them materials had to take anything he could find and this included engravings. All of the Clews assets were sold in 1835. Ralph retired to the country.

Then in 1836 James Clews came to Louisville, Kentucky at the invitation of Samuel Casseday, a Louisville importer of earthenware. In 1837 the Indiana Pottery Company was formed by Jacob Lewis, a potter, Samuel Casseday and Clews. Louisville business men raised the money because they believed that a viable pottery could compete with the Staffordshire imports and create a source of pottery in America. The site was chosen at Troy, Indiana as it was believed that the proper clay and coal would be available there. Clews brought in 36 potters from England and production began; the wares were marked with Clews name and the words "Manufactury", because of his fame.

In 1838 the company was in trouble. No additional craftsmen could be trained quickly, the expense of importing labor was huge and the managers realized that the pottery would operate at a loss for a very long time. Clews stayed in Troy where he had purchased land in 1838, but left in 1842 after selling his shares in the venture back to the company. He went to New York City and stayed there until 1847 when he sold his land in Troy. Records show that he was in England in 1849, living near Stoke-On-Trent.

James Clews, great potter, a venturesome man willing to travel to a strange country, helping to set up a brave new business, died at home in England at age 71. After all the disappointments and near disasters one hopes that he realized that he was no failure. His works remain to attest his success.

*See Bibliography "English Pottery and Porcelain".

**Other marks were also used and many are illustrated in this book.

PLATE II

James Clews
Oil impression by JoCleta Wilson, Kentucky.

Floral Category

ALBERT

Made by John Meir & Son

A sprawling design of daffodils crosses the face of this dish. The lower left part of the rim is covered with large water lilies and a spray of ferns. A butterfly is placed at top right.

Marked I.M. & S. Like GMK. 2639, c. 1837-97.

AMULA

Made by Edward Challinor & Co.

The dark stippled rim of this plate is contained by a wreath of scrolls on the cavetto. Four roses alternate with four morning-glories around the border. In the center scene a vase is at left, a tall peony rises at center and there are over-scaled peony-type flowers and leaves in the foreground. This plate is multi-colored; the border is very dark green, and the other colors used are red and yellow. The design on the cup plate repeats the central vase and flower motifs.

Marked E. Challinor & Co., GMK. 836, 1853-62.

AVON

Maker unknown

The rim of this soup dish is covered with a bold design of morning-glories, tendrils, furled leaves and single wheat heads. In the center an ornate dark urn contains an overscaled bouquet and overscaled flowers are placed at left and on the base. A butterfly is at upper right. This plate is multi-colored and is overprinted with green, red and blue.

"BOTANICAL PATTERN" NUMBER 13

Made by Copeland and Garrett

The evenly scalloped white edge of this dish is detailed with a narrow band of dark beads and bars separated by pairs of bell flowers. The concave stippled rim is decorated with three different floral sprays separated by horn-like designs of foliated scrolls and blossoms. The border design covers the cavetto and enters the well where it is contained by a wreath of scrolls and ovals.

The central design consists of two large astor-like flowers with serrated leaves and some buds.

Marked as above with the words "New Blanche" GMK. 1091, c. 1833-47.

CANELLA

Made by Edward Challinor

*The panelled rim of this saucer is covered with a stippled background.
A design of four large foliated white scrolls set over pairs of small stylized
white flowers alternates with four pairs of large prunus and leaves set under
a single elongated foliated scroll.*

*A band of striated floral brocade interrupted at four points by a rosette
flanked by scrolls and a fleur-de-lis encircles the central floral picture. Part
of a basket can be seen at left and a large foliated scroll design supports a
bouquet of over-scaled lilies, forget-me-nots and cabbage roses. A smaller
flower and bud are placed under the basket section. This dish is printed in
dark green and the floral designs are polychrome.*

Marked E. Challinor, G.M.K. c. 1842-67.

FLORALIA

Maker unknown

The edge of this hot water dish is trimmed with a wreath of snail-like sprigged curves. The upper rim is covered with narrow vertical lines over a stippled background. The border design consists of fans composed of speckled oval shapes flared around dark reserves containing a serrated leaf. The fans alternate with triangular bouquets surmounted by small birds. In the center a woven straw basket with a tall handle is filled with large flowers. The border design on the base is different and consists of foliated scrolls and flowers set against a dark ground.

GERANIUM

Made by Deakin & Son

The edge of this plate is lobed in six places which are indicated on the face by printed beads flanked by scrolls at the upper edge which is embossed and decorated with a ribbon band. Three large groups of purple geraniums are placed around the rim and well.

Marked D. & S. and (imp.) "Deakin Pearl". Mark not listed, see Godden page 195. 1833-41.

HAWTHORNE
Made by Livesley Powell & Co.

Coysh calls this type of design a sheet pattern. The dish is covered with a repetitive design of small circular white reserves filled with either roses or hawthorne blossoms and separated by seaweed. It is printed in mulberry and blue.

Marked L.P. & Co. and Ironstone, GMK. 2386, c. 1851-66.

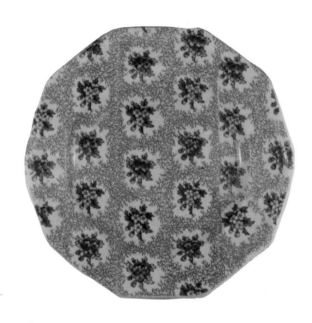

HAWTHORN BLOSSOM

Made by Samuel Alcock & Co.

Clumps of pale mulberry blossoms, framed by ferns, are placed around the face of the saucer shown. The scalloped edge of the dish is decorated with a scalloped band edged with beads, small dotted circles and tiny fleur-de-lis.

Marked (ptd.) Sm & Co., and (imp.) Alcock and a behive, like GMK. 75, 1830-59.

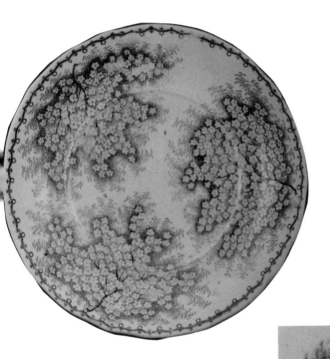

HOLLYHOCK

Maker unknown

The background of this dish is stippled and is greyish blue. The white hollyhock design spreads across the entire dish.

HYBLA

Made by Brougham & Mayer

The edge of the panelled rim of this saucer is decorated with a wreath of laurel leaves and berries. A band is placed around the middle of the rim. Three pairs of flowers surrounded by sprigs and buds alternate on the band with a bow-like design of double ovals centered with a small rose, dark leaves and buds. The designs are joined by garlands of leaves. In the center a basket placed on a stone shelf is filled with over-scaled peonies, roses, leaves, sprays and buds.

Hybla is a town in Sicily named for the Greek word for "sweet" and is renowned for its bees.

Marked as above. GMK. 649, c. 1853-5.

31

JAPAN DAISY

Made by John Wedge Wood

Large fern fronds, seaweed and lacy sprigs centered with pairs of exotic flowers are placed around the concave rim of this unevenly scalloped soup dish. The central design which almost covers the well consists of a whirling bouquet of the same exotic plants. The design on the cup plate appears only on the rim.

Marked J. Wedgwood, See GMK. 4276A, c. 1841-60.

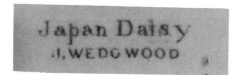

JAVA

Made by Charles Meigh & Son

A band of beads is placed around the edge of this soup plate. The band is interrupted by three pairs of large peony-like flowers that alternate with three open ovals formed by beaded curves. In each oval there is a small posy, and sprays from the ovals cover the rest of the rim. A wreath of beaded scallops interspersed by three half-flowers covers the cavetto. In the center two large peonies are placed above a beaded double scroll and the small flowers repeated from the rim pattern are placed at right.

Marked C.M. & S., like GMK. 2620, 1851-61.

JESSEMINE

Maker unknown

This deep saucer is covered with a sheet pattern of sprawling curved sprigs. The stippled background is printed in a medium blue with a lavender cast. The flowers are white with white stems outlined in dark blue. A band of dark centered white beads encircles the edge of the dish.

MADRAS

Made by Davenport

These dishes are gently scalloped and the edges are outlined by a band of trailing leaves. The border wreath consists of flowers of oriental patterns such as seen in the Indian Tree patterns. A jagged band of leaves surrounds the center medallion of a pair of flowers and leaves. This design is printed in cobalt with a slight flown quality. Also shown are a pitcher with mask-head spout and a soup tureen.

Marked (imp.) as above, GMK. 1181A, dated 1844.

MADRAS (cont.)

NANKEEN

Attributed to Andrew Stevenson

The edge of this dish is gently lobed and the upper rim is covered with a pattern of small six-petalled white flowers and scrolls set against a dark background. Six large stylized blossoms consisting of five petals are set around the rim and floral aprons descend from these to a brocade band placed around a central basket of oriental flowers. Bouquets of the same type of flowers are placed in the reserves formed by the apron panels.

Exact mark, GMK. 3702, c. 1816-30.

NEVA

Made by Edward Challinor

This pattern is printed in dark sepia. The border pattern on the octagonal dish consists of a wreath of arches. Small dark stylized four petal flowers and sprigs are placed around the upper rim between the arches. Curlicue pendants descend from the flowers. The same four-petal flowers, although smaller, are placed in the arches, and each has a curled stem. The large blossoms in the center resemble poppies. Shadow sprays of bell flowers are placed behind the blossoms

Marked E. Challinor, GMK. 1835A, c. 1842-67.

NYMPH

Mark not located

   This dish is part of a child's tea set. It is printed in lavender and consists of water lilies in a wreath around the border with two large flower buds and pads in the center.
   Marked H.W.

PERSIAN ROSE

Mark not located

The edge of this gently scalloped dish is defined by a wreath of dark scrolls and buds that contains small flowers. The scrolls form shallow arches which are separated by a diamond and arrow pendant. The concave paneled rim is decorated with a smaller floral spray across the cavetto. The Rose of the title is at center. It is surrounded by buds, small flowers and leaves. The transfer print is lavender and the flowers are polychromed.

Marked M.T.

ROSE

Maker unknown

This twelve-sided plate is printed in mulberry. The border design consists of a wreath of small berries and dark leaves on an angled vine which is also covered with small three-petalled flowers.

A large open rose on a curved stem with large leaves is in the center of the dish and on its left there is a bouquet of small flowers and buds.

Marked Real Ironstone.

(Jacob Furnival used the term "Real Ironstone" (1845-70). See Rose (The) by Thomas Furnival, this book. The plates are made on the same mold and the central pattern is the same. This could be a Furnival product.)

ROSE (THE)

Made by Thomas Furnival

This plate is twelve-sided and the edges are detailed with a band of small white arches set under darts. The panelled rim is decorated with sprays of rosebuds.

A full blown rose is placed across the center of the dish. Other flowers are placed at left. This pattern is printed in lavender and over-painted with natural colors under the glaze.

Marked T.F. & Co., GMK. 1645, c. 1844-6.

ROSETTA

Made by Edward Challinor

The panelled rim of the dish photographed is covered with three bands. The upper and lower are composed of narrow lines. The center ribbon is stippled and six pairs of flowers with sprigs and leaves are placed on this band. The border is finished on the cavetto with a wreath of small bars and triangles.

A pair of roses is set on a circle in the center of the dish. A wreath of narrow lines form a large circle around the flowers, and in turn is enclosed by a band of curved triangles and diamonds that resemble Moorish motifs.

ROSETTE

Made by George Wooliscroft

    The panelled rim of this plate is covered with a design of triple bars that curve and form ornate reserves containing pairs of flowers with leaves and a scrolled keyhole design. The uppermost part of the rim is dark and carries four foliated scrolls above the floral patterns. A pair of large roses with many buds flanked by large leaves is placed in the center.

    Marked G. Wooliscroft, GMK. 4308, c. 1851-64.

"ROSETTE WREATH"

Made by John and George Alcock

This scalloped cup plate has a concave rim that is covered with a wreath of small rosettes with fine sprigs and small six-petalled star-like flowers with tendrils. The center medallion is composed of a smaller version of the rosettes.

Marked (imp.) J. and G. Alcock, and Cobridge, GMK. 68, c. 1839-46.

SHIRAZ

Made by John Ridgway

The scalloped edge of this dish is white and a narrow black line of fringe accents the scallops. The rim is concave and panelled. The rim design consists of four scroll-framed vignettes which feature a small oriental sailboat manned by two men in peaked hats. In the background one sees temples and bamboo trees. The reserves are separated by garlands of white roses. The border design invades the well and is contained by a narrow twisted ribbon inset with rosettes.

A bouquet placed on a large scrolled base fills the center of the dish. This plate is printed in sepia and the border is pale creamy gold. Shiraz is a city in Iran (formerly Persia).

Marked J.R., GMK. 3253, c. 1830-55.

SNOW DROP
Mark not located

The urn photographed bears a diaper design of white crosses and quatre-foils against a stippled ground. A band of spearpoint contains the border pattern.

In the center of the well and on the outside of the urn there is a picture of a basket with a tall handle filled with flowers and sprigs. A band of spearpoint is placed around the bottom of the pedestal base.

Marked Y. and M.

SOUVENIR

Made by John Ridgway & Co.

The edge of this square tureen stand is scalloped and is decorated by a band of oval cartridge forms placed over a band of small beads. Horizontal reserves are formed on the rim by short vertical columns decorated with twelve ovate stylized daisies. A band of narrow bell-like flowers and beads encloses the bottom of the reserves and forms a wreath around the dish. This band is interrupted by floral sprays that extend from the bottom of the columns. In each reserve there are three flowers, leaves and sprays set in a small basket that looks like a cornucopia.

The central rococo bouquet design is formed of lattice and scrolls. There is a crown near the base that is placed under the bouquet of flowers and leaves.

Marked *Jn° Ridgway & Co., GMK. 3258, (Unusual printed date "No. 692 10th, May 1841").*

SOUVENIR (cont.)

SPANISH ROSE

Made by Davenport

The edge of this mulberry, white and gilt dish is outlined by a band of white beads interspersed at five points by pairs of short scrolls flanking a triangle which gives the effect of s script letter "M". Pairs of roses are placed around the concave rim between the scroll designs. The roses of the title sprawl across the face of the plate.

Marked as above and also with (imp.) anchor GMK. 1181A, Dated 1848.

SPANISH ROSE (cont.)

SYDENHAM

Maker unknown

This ten-sided plate has an embossed groove around the edge. The upper part of the concaved panelled rim is stippled and is decorated with white foliated scrolls. Six large flowers enhanced by little buds and sprigs are placed around the border.

In the center three large flowers form a bouquet that is flanked by dark veined leaves, sprigs and buds.

TUSCAN ROSE

Made by James and Ralph Clews

This pattern was presented in Book 1 on page 51 but that dish was made by John and William Ridgway. Note that the string of beads around the central scene are omitted in the Clews version. A cup plate and a relish dish are pictured.

Marked as above, (imp.), GMK. 919, c. 1818-34.

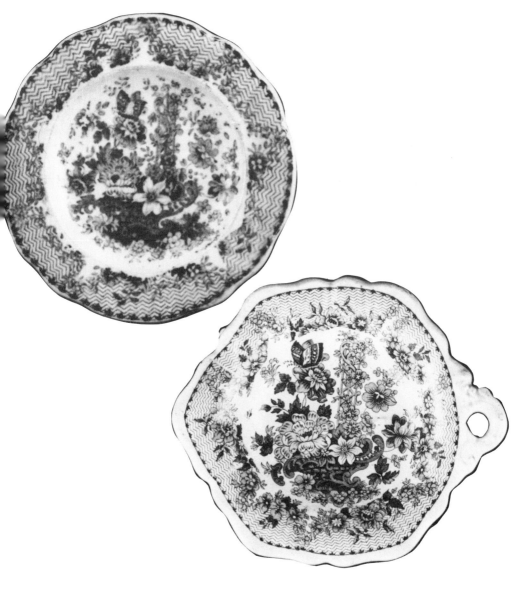

WILD FLOWERS

Made by Thomas Dimmock

   The unevenly scalloped edge of this soup plate is outlined in tan luster by a trailing vine. White enamel is then placed in an embossed circle of scallops with fringe of uneven lengths. Six different sprays of wild flowers are placed around the green rim in the arches formed by the white enamel wreath. The well is covered by a bold sepia design of ferns, wild roses, poppy-like flowers and bell flowers, stems and leaves.
   Marked D. & Kaolin, GMK. 1298, c. 1844-59.

"WINDSOR ROSE"

Made by William Adams & Sons

The concave rim of this scalloped pink and white cup plate is covered with large open roses, rose buds and leaves, sprigs and small bunches of grapes. The center transfer fills the well and consists of a single full-blown rose with its leaves and two buds, set against fruits and a pair of small five-petalled flowers.

Marked (imp.) Adams, GMK. 18, c. 1830-40.

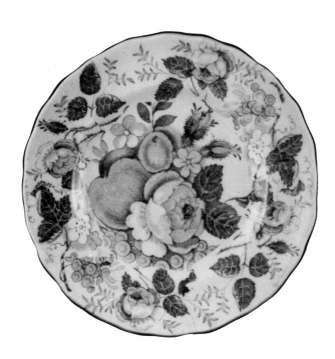

Classical Category

CARRARA

Made by John Holland

The panelled concave rim of this saucer is covered with a diaper design composed of rounded diamonds intersected by narrow concenctric lines. This pattern is contained at the top by three narrow dark bands which are interrupted by six scroll fleur-de-lis. The same dark bands are at the bottom of the border and enclose a wreath of scalloped swags and diamonds.

The central picture presents a terrace in a formal garden. A large statue of a woman, a girl and a greyhound is at right next to a pair of pedestals supporting dark urns. In the left foreground there is a part of a balustrade and in the distance one sees a lake, some castle towers and distant mountains.

Marked J. Holland, Reg. Nov. 1852 GMK. 2060, c. 1852-4.

CLASSICAL ANTIQUITIES

Made by Joseph Clementson

The four dishes photographed bear the same border of reserves filled with Grecian urns and fruit-filled compotes which are separated by foliated scrolls that meet at the upper rim above the urn designs. The entire background of the pale green plates is stippled and the transfer pattern is white. The center scenes are framed by a wreath of leaves and tendrils. The first dish shows the great Greek poet Homer listening to the muse of poetry. It is entitled "Homer Invokes the Muse." The second dish is titled "Juno's Command," and shows the seated Goddess instructing a young girl who sits on the floor beside her. The third plate shows Ulysses seated at right, wearing his traveller's cap, cloak and short boots. He holds a towel to his eyes. The plate title is "Ulysses Weeps at the Song of Demodocus." A platter from this series printed in blue is shown in Book I, page 65. The fourth plate is also blue and is entitled "Phemius Singing to the Suitors."

Marked J. Clementson, GMK. 910A, dated 1840.

CLASSICAL ANTIQUITIES (cont.)

CLASSICAL ANTIQUITIES (cont.)

ETRUSCAN VASE

Maker unknown

This cup plate is printed in light blue. The vase of the title is at center. It is surrounded by sprigs and there are small flowers and feathers at its base. Sprigs are placed around the rim in three places and the scalloped edge is defined by a narrow band of fringe.

Marked with a beehive, might be Samuel Alcock.

ESTRUSCAN VASES
Maker unknown

The dishes shown are gently scalloped and the edges are detailed by a row of white beads. The rim design of wild roses, dark leaves and faint white scrolls on a stippled background covers the concave rim and enters the cavetto. It is contained in the well by a wreath of feathery scrolls. Both dishes show a tall stand of hollyhocks at right and a tree with a white gnarled base and many leaves at left. Each scene is dominated by a vase on a pedestal in the left foreground. The flowers around the vases are the same but the designs of the large vases differ as do the backgrounds that show different buildings beyond the river.

GRECIAN STATUE
Made by Wood & Brownfield

The cup plate shown has a border pattern of small five-petalled flowers interspersed in four places with a large flower with dark leaves. The scalloped edge is decorated with a band of white ovals containing darts. The statue of the warrior of the title set on a decorated wide plinth is in the center of the scene; there are shadowy elms behind the figure and towered buildings in the left background. The cup plate is printed in light blue.

The border is different on the large (10″) Flow Blue plate. The same little five petalled flowers form frames for the medallions on the stippled rim, three which are circular and show urns and flowers, and three which are oval and picture towered buildings. The reserves are separated by large flowers with dark leaves set on triangular vase forms. The small flowers coupled with scrolls form a wreath around the cavetto.

The statue of the title is again prominent and in the center of the scene. There are elms and vases at right, parts of broken columns and parts of broken statues in the foreground. In the background there is a river with a boat on it, some trees, and in the distance at left there are towers.

Marked W. & B. GMK. 4242, c. 1838-50.

65

LOUVRE
Maker unknown

The white edge of this unevenly scalloped plate is enhanced by a narrow band of white embossed roping. A printed wider band of rope bound with criss-cross ties and decorated with rosettes follows the scallop pattern. In the arches formed by the above, large open roses and passion flowers alternate with trophy designs of torches and curved hunting horns. The bottom of all these elements covers the cavetto and forms an irregular wreath around the well.

A statue of a goddess stands near the foreground which is covered with roses, flowers and ferns. At the extreme right there is an urn on a pedestal and tall elms. At extreme left there is a statue of a female head on a low pedestal and tall trees rise behind the bust. In the distance one sees a lake, a classical mansion and tall mountains.

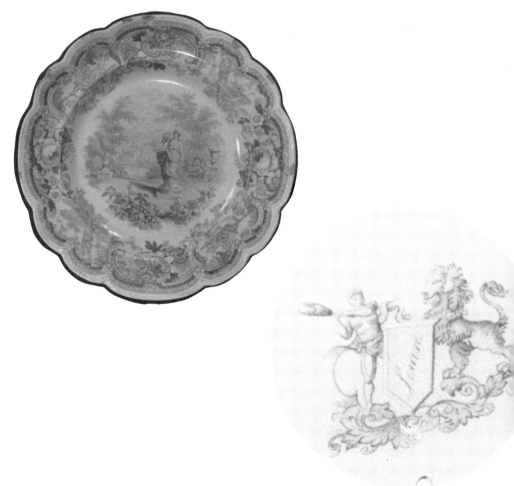

NEAPOLITAN

Made by Thomas Dimmock

The edge of this scalloped green plate is decorated with a band of white beads that contain dark diamonds. A white diaper pattern of ovals descends from the band and covers the stippled background. Six classical urns filled with flowers alternate on the border with pairs of flowers that includes passion flowers, large cabbage roses, asters and dahlias. A wide wreath of lacy springs on the cavetto frames the center scene. In the left foreground there is a statue of a seated woman in Greek clothing. She sits with her hand on an urn and leans against a pedestal base. A tall elm rises at right and in the background, across the lake, there is a mansion with columned portico. In the distance there are a fountain, a temple and mountain peaks.

Marked D and Stoneware like GMK. 1299, dated 1828-59.

PARMA

Made by Powell and Bishop

This lavender cake plate has a border of rose-filled medallions separated by horizontal sprays of roses, leaves and sprigs. The outer edge is decorated with printed white scallops in a stippled ground. The border is contained in the cavetto by a wreath of hairpin ovals and spearpoint.

In the central scene a very large urn is set at left upon a table-like pedestal. The vase is decorated with a scene of dancing women and it holds roses and trailing vines and leaves that arch over the center of the picture. Overscaled roses are placed in the left foreground and surround the pedestal. There is a squat dark urn with large round handles set upon the end of a balustrade at right. A tall slender arch rises against some elms at right and a similar arch is in the center background.

Marked P & B and (imp.) a caduceus GMK. 3132 and 3135, c. 1876.

Oriental Category

ABBEVILLE

Probably made by Samuel Alcock

The fourteen sided plate photographed was made with a panelled concave rim. The upper part of the rim is covered with concentric narrow lines, and small diamonds form a diaper pattern with the lines. Fourteen white fleur-de-lis are placed around the outer edge. The narrow white lines connect the fleur-de-lis and contain the diaper pattern. The lower border pattern is composed of a wide scrolled ribbon band, decorated acanthus leaves and stylized passion flowers. Small flowers are placed above and below the band of scrolls. Lacey swags placed around the cavetto form an irregular wreath around the well.

The central scene appears to be tropical. A tall palm tree is at right and a smaller one is placed at left across the river that divides the scene. A pavilion with curved roof is in the background near the middle of the picture. Abbeville probably was a French settlement in North Africa.

Marked *"Florentine China"* and a beehive, c. 1828-59.

ARABIAN SKETCHES

Possibly made by William Hackwood

The white edge of this scalloped plate is enhanced by a wreath of small rosettes and tiny beads. The stippled concave rim presents three scenic vignettes, each showing the same scene of a turreted castle at left, a river in the center, an arched bridge and a small stone building and tall trees at right. The scenes are joined by four foliated framed ovals containing four different blossoms. There are sprigs beneath the ovals. The rim pattern is contained at the top of the cavetto by a white scalloped band, and vertical floral and oak leaf strips descend from the scallops into the well.

In the central scene there are two figures in the foreground. One man is dressed in a Spanish jacket, hat and knee breeches. He is seated on a black horse and points toward the river that flows at left. The other man is wearing a fur bordered cape and short boots, carrying a lance and has dismounted from his white steed which he holds by its halter. The plate shown is lavender. It is subtitled "The March."

Marked W.H., GMK. 1886, c. 1827-43.

ASIATIC PALACES

Made by Ridgways

Some of the dark blue and white dishes in this pattern are scalloped and circular and some are octagonal. All have a gadroon white edge. The border design crosses the cavetto and enters the well where it is confined by a band of small white scallops crowned with beads and tiny fleur-de-lis. The rim is covered with a wreath of large white dahlia-type flowers which alternate with a passion flower. The flower and leaf design are separated by a small rosette flanked by scrolls. The background is stippled.

The scenes differ as shown on these plates. The larger plate, which is scalloped, pictures a double arched bridge in the foreground. Three little figures wearing triangular Chinese hats are on the bridge. There are temples at left, a river with a sampan at right. A tall bamboo rises from some rocks at center. There are low rounded hills in the background.

The other scalloped plate shows the small figures on a mound in the foreground. A large vase is at left. It is filled with overscaled flowers. There are temples at right. A river with a boat on it is shown at center.

The small octagonal plates show respectively a large temple at the center foreground, an overscaled flower arrangement at right, a temple, water and mountains in the background.

This is a late mark (pre 1891). Mark not photographed. Pattern is included in this book as it may have been a reissue.

ASIATIC PALACES (cont.)

ASIATIC TEMPLES
Made by John & William Ridgway

The damaged teapot photographed was the only example located before publication. It is dark blue. The rim design is composed of stylized flowers. The central design is surrounded by a wreath of small crosses and shows two small buildings at left with curved roofs and two pagoda towers in the right distance.

Marked J.W.R., GMK. 3260, c. 1814-1830.

"BASKET AND VASE"

Made by Francis Morley

The rim of this little (5") plate is decorated with a band of trefoils and single beads. The border design consists of three sprays of flowers and leaves that differ from each other in small details. The basket of the title is set upon a small taboret at left. It has a tall handle topped with a bow and is filled with small flowers. The vase is at right and it is supporting an over-scaled peony with its buds and dark leaves. The transfer is in light sepia and the flowers are over coloured with pastels.

Marked (imp.) FM, GMK. 2759, 1845-58.

CANDIA

Mady by John Ridgway & Co.

The upper part of the panelled rim of this saucer is covered with a diaper pattern that resembles snail-scrolls. Moorish arches enclose large peonies and alternate with a stylized bud flanked by scrolls around the border of the dish. In the center, there is a large flower, a peony or chrysanthemum set over a box or a brush case.

Marked J.R. & Co., GMK. 3259, c. 1841-5.

"CANTON" No. 107
Made by Enoch Wood & Sons

This stippled rim of this unevenly scalloped multicoloured dish is covered with small flowers and sprigs. The outer edge is decorated with a band of sprigs. Three pairs of large flowers, flanked by a spray of bell flowers at right and a wild rose at left, alternate with pairs of crossed ostrich feathers, which on this plate have been overcolored. A wreath of forget-me-nots encircles the cavetto.

The central scene pictures a kneeling woman in long gown, apron and pointed triangular hat who is planting flowers into an urn. A small figure in pantaloons and Chinese cap stands near her. In the background, behind a wall, there is an oriental temple with an awning and a large decorated epi on top of the tower section. At left there are palm trees.

A different central scene was used on the blue plate shown in the Scenic section of Book I page 427, and catalogued under the name "Swiss". That scene may have been intended to be Oriental also, but it contains Alpine peaks in the distance.

Marked E. Wood & Sons and No. 107, GMK. 4261, c. 1818-46.

CASHMERE

Made by Francis Morley

The rim of this plate is printed with mauresque lambrequins separated by half of a sunflower at the top. The pattern is famous for its center scene of two little deer, one with antlers, that confront each other with upraised front legs. There is an overscaled peony tree at right which arises from some rock forms. This printing is in pale blue; the pattern is famous in Flow Blue. Marked F.M. & Co., GMK. 2760, c. 1845-58.

CASHMERE (cont.)

CHIAN

Made by Davenport

   The panelled rim of this fourteen sided plate is covered with a tracery of leaf shapes and vines set over a background of narrow concentric lines. The outer edge is detailed with a row of beads and the bottom of the border is contained by a wreath of small scallops and beads. The central scene of Chinoiserie shows a small open garden house perched on a mound. Two small figures are sitting beneath the curved roof. There are rock forms on either side of the structure. A tall tree rises from the right and arches over the scene. A second small open tea house is across the ravine or stream at left.

   Marked as above, GMK. 1181A, dated 1844.

CHIANG

Mark not located.

The bowl photographed has tab handles and was used for ice or butter. The pattern on the outer sides consists of a fancy dark urn decorated with the white figures of two women, and at right a square fenced enclosure that surrounds an overscaled peony tree. The border pattern appears in the top inside rim and is composed of pairs of dark scrolls which flank a bellflower and which are crowned by the half of a dark daisy. These are separated by a fan-like design with a pebbled border surrounding a half of a white six petalled blossom set over a smaller blue flower. This pattern was made in Flow Blue by Wood and Brownfield and named "Japanese" and was dated 1875.

Marked J.G.

CHIANG (cont.)

"CHINESE EXPORT BOAT PATTERN"
Made by John & William Ridgway

This small blue and white plate is an early copy of the wares sent to England in the days of the China trade. It is slightly lobed and the concave rim is covered at top with a diamond diaper trellis design. The lowest section of the rim contains a wreath of dagger point.

A sail boat, in the left foreground, is pulled up to shore beneath a fenced Oriental mansion. An apple tree is at right, a willow at left. In the background there is another small boat at left, and across a large body of water there are an island and a mountain. A flight of small birds form a "V" at upper right.

Marked J.&W. Ridgway, GMK. 3262, c. 1814-30.

CHINESE GEM
Made by Troutbeck

A band of arches contains the upper rim design of pairs of white griffons on this bowl. Leonine masks are set in six dark reserves between the griffons and alternate with shield-shaped scrolled reserves crowned with a white acanthus. Scrolls and leaves connect the design below the dark band. The border pattern is classic in design. A wide band of scrolls, three large Greek or Oriental key designs and three shields form a frame for the central scene of a large pagoda, wide steps, and a terrace. A man holding a spear and a lady holding a parasol stand in the foreground on a paved terrace. At left there is a body of water upon which a sampan sails towards the pagoda. In the distance at left there is a mountain peak and upon the peak there is a tower surmounted by a large pennant.

The cup plate shown has the same border as the bowl but a narrow string of crosses and bars contains the border design at the base of the cavetto. The central scene is almost the same as that of the bowl with the exception that the arches in the left background are fewer and shorter than in the larger design.

Marked MT&T. Also found marked Troutbeck, Tunstall. The marks are not located.

CHINESE PAGODA
Made by Elkin, Knight and Bridgwood

The collar of the pitcher shown is probably trimmed with the same pattern or part of the pattern used on the rims of plates in this design. The outer white edge is detailed with a band of oval beads. The upper part of the border is stippled and is covered with a diamond diaper pattern. The crossed lines forming the diamonds are decorated with rosettes. The stippled section is contained by a series of scrolls. Pairs of large flowers alternate with a single large blossom in reserves formed under the scrolls by vertical scrolled bars.

The pagoda of the title is set at the top of a flight of curved steps. Three little people are on the porch of the open pagoda. In the foreground there are three other figures; one holds a pipe, one holds a stick with bells, the other sits on the ground. They are placed on a fenced terrace. A tall spray of flowers is at right and overscaled flowers are in the foreground. At left there is another tall spray of flowers and in the background there is a building with a spire. In the distance one sees water and mountains.

Marked E.K.B., GMK. 1464, c. 1827-40.

CHINESE PAGODA AND BRIDGE

Maker Unknown

The large dish shown is scalloped and has a white embossed gadroon edge. The cup plate is slightly scalloped and its dark edge is decorated with printed shell forms linked by white stringing. The border pattern (detail illustrated) consists of four large foliated shields enclosing a Chinese key design and a diamond. These alternate with floral sprays.

A delicate circle of scallops and triangles frames the central scenes. The large plate presents the pagoda of the title in the center background. The bridge is in the foreground and crosses a small stream which flows between mossy banks and large rocks. There are a large pine tree and tall elms at right and in the distance there are islands, water and mountains. Only the bridge, the rocks and the foliage covered banks are shown on the cup plate. There is a shadowy large building in the right background and there are mountains and water in the distance. The plate is printed in dark blue and the cup plate is black and white.

CHINESE PAGODA AND BRIDGE (cont.)

CHINESE ROSE

Made by Davenport

Four triangular scrolled fence designs alternate with four peony and bud patterns around the rim of this saucer. In the center of the dish two angled sections of trellis fence set upon a platform enclose an overscaled peony tree. A lotus bud is at right; at left there are two birds, one in flight and the other perched on a sprig.

Marked as above. GMK. 1179A, c. 1820-60.

"CHINESE TEA GARDEN"

Made by Robert Cochran & Co.

The tureen stand pictured here bears a rim design of large peonies and pairs of dahlia-like flowers connected by leafy branches and three long foliated rococo scrolls. The upper part of the rim is black. The transfer print is grey.

In the center, a small crested bird sits on the limb of a flowering peony tree. An overscaled blossom is at the tree base. There are rock forms, pebbles, and flowers in the foreground. A fence crosses the background and encloses an open pavilion and a garden. There are three bamboo trees behind the pavilion.

Marked (imp.) R.C. & Co. and improved Stone China, GMK. 965, 1846 plus.

"CHINESE TEMPLES"

Made by Davenport

The white edge of this scalloped dish is elaborated with embossed triangular floral groups set at eight places around the plate. The border design is placed between the white flowers and consists of dark foliated scrolls at the top and pale floral sprays beneath them. A wreath of diamonds and stars encircles the central scene which is dominated by a large temple with tall towers at each end of its extensive length. It is set upon a platform high above the water on an island. A bridge connects the island to the bank at right, and there are large rocks, overscaled flowers, and a tall elm in the right foreground. In the background there is a river with a junk sailing between islands and there are mountains in the distance.

Marked as above. Exact GMK. 1185, c. 1820-60.

"CHINESE TEMPLES"

Made by Wood and Challinor

This same blue and white pattern was made by Davenport and is shown in the preceding picture. The central scene differs in small details. The temple is of a different structure and the elm is placed nearer the center. It may be that the center scenes differ on most of these dishes.

Marked as above. Like mark 4245, c. 1828-43.

CHINESE VIEWS

Made by Edward and George Phillips

The scalloped edge of this blue printed plate is white and is embossed. The upper stippled rim is covered with small stylized flowers and sprigs and at six points there are large flowers. The stippled design extends into triangles towards the well. In the arches thus created are shadowy sprays, each different from the other. The arches are joined at the cavetto by a pale floral band.

The central scene presents a double roofed island pavilion in the middle ground. Stairs pass under an arch in the entrance to the building. There is a boat on the water at right. A tall palm tree rises at left and there are rocks and sprigs and water in the foreground.

Marked E.&G. Phillips, GMK. 3009, c. 1822-34.

CIRCASSIA

Made by John and George Alcock

    The upper part of the cobalt border of this saucer is very dark, almost black. Foliated scrolls and small flowers connect the large six-petalled flowers and the scroll heart-shaped design and large peonies around the middle of the rim. These are set against a stippled background. The central scene shows ornate temples on either side of a river. There are stylized rock forms in the foreground and a slender peony tree rises from the rocks.

    Marked J.&G. Alcock, Cobridge (imp.) Oriental Stone, GMKS. 68 and 69, c. 1839-46.

COLANDINE

Mark not located

A band of scalloped fencing is placed around the stippled edge of the plate shown. The fencing dips into scrolls at three spots and forms oval reserves containing stylized flowers. Small sprigs extend from the bottom of the reserves. Large peonies alternate with the reserves.

In the central scene a small male figure is on the steps of an ornate temple at left. At right there are rock forms, overscaled flowers and leaves. In the background at right there are a small garden house and a tall flowering tree. The details of the transfer are highly stylized.

Marked R.F.F.T.

"CRANE AND PEONY TREE"
Made by Davenport

The edge of this lobed dish is gilded and a band of small fleur-de-lis is set around the top of the concaved rim. Three long sprays of prunus separate the three pictures of a duck or goose walking in a puddle. A ring of inverted fleur-de-lis is around the cavetto. A crane stands on an angled platform at left. A tall peony tree rises at right and arches over the bird. The transfer is blue and the details are colored with navy, red, purple, light blue and much gold outlining. This pattern was used by Clews in a blue printing with a different border. See Book I page 119.

Marked Davenport, Stone China, GMK. 1183, c. 1805-20.

DELHI

Maker Unknown

The scalloped edge of this dish is decorated with a band of small white quatrefoil beads. The border design consists of six vertical Gothic scroll designs that separate six floral reserves containing exotic lilies. Beneath the rim pattern there is a wreath of dotted thick scrolls that flank six stylized half-floral forms. Beneath each vertical scroll there are pendent beads, diamonds and quatrefoils that enter the well.

The central scene is dominated by a large Egyptian temple in the center. In the background at left there are buildings and two pyramids. At right one sees other buildings, palm trees and a mountain. A man standing in the foreground holds a rifle and is talking to a seated man. They are near a bank surmounted by a century plant. At left there is a tall bushy tree. This pattern is reputed to have been made by Adams but a marked example could not be located.

"DIAMOND SUNBURST BORDER"

Probably made by Enoch Wood & Sons

This pattern is shown as an unknown scenic design on page 711 of Vol. I. That saucer is printed with a red border and a green center. The saucer photographed here has a blue border and a sepia central scene. It bears the same picture of Chinese figures in a little boat and an oriental temple in the right background.

Marked (imp.) Wood, GMK. 4247, 1818-46.

ERFORD

Probably made by James Edwards

The rim of this fourteen sided plate is covered with a pattern of rounded lyre-like forms connected at top, bottom and middle with foliated short scrolls set against a black background that is sprinkled with white dots. A wreath of scrolls, bellflowers and fleur-de-lis encircles the cavetto.

The central scene pictures an open temple and its court. The upturned roof is draped with little bells. There are bamboo trees and part of an elm behind the structure. At left across a river there is a pagoda on a hill and mountain peaks in the distance.

Marked Jas. Edwards and "Real Ironstone", See Godden, bottom page 230, c. 1842-51.

ERICA

Made by Davenport

The toy dishes photographed are printed in green. The full border pattern appears on the soup plate. Three cartouches containing dark floral patterns are separated by trailing vines, fuschia blossoms and small buds. A band of pairs of leaves and beaded double hooks encircle the outer edge. The central transfer pictures a pavilion with tall tower at right, a river, and an island with pagoda at left. A sampan is near the island. A man and woman stand on a fenced terrace in the middle of the scene.

The smaller dish carries only the vine design on its rim. In the center a gardener pushes a wheel barrow. In the left background there is a tall gate with upturned roof. At right there are tall bamboo trees. A river and small boat are in the background and in the distance there are a tower and other buildings.

Marked (Ptd. and imp.), Davenport, GMK. 1181a, dated 1844. (Dishes from the collection of Louise Loehr)

ERICA (cont.)

INDIAN BRIDGE

Made by Samuel Alcock & Co.

The panelled rim of this twelve sided dish is decorated with opposing pairs of stylized chrysanthemums and lotus. A band of brocade inset with oval and circular reserves covers the cavetto. The bridge of the title is in the foreground. A tall stylized tree rises on either side of the central picture behind the bridge.

Marked S.A. & Co. GMK. 75, c. 1830-59.

INDIAN JAR

Made by Jacob & Thomas Furnival

The octagonal platter photographed printed in dark sepia carries an upper border pattern of triangular wing-like designs crowned with a half sunflower which alternate with rounded wings filled with circular diapering. The designs are linked by small garlands. A band of brocade, composed of the same circular diaper pattern inset with floral oblongs, frames the central picture. The jar of the title is at left. It is placed on a pedestal table with scrolled feet. Overscaled flowers are placed on the table at right. An oblong box and small vase are on the flat lid of the Indian jar. This pattern was also made in Flow Blue.

Marked J.&T.F., GMK. 1644, c. 1843.

INDIAN TEMPLES
Maker Unknown

A plate in this pattern is shown in Book I on page 297, in the Scenic category. It should be catalogued in the Oriental category. The plate is unevenly scalloped and the outer edge is white. A row of small printed diamonds follows the scalloped outline. The rim bears three baroque cartouches framed in scrolls and draped with small flowers. Each contains a distinctive picture of an open air temple with peaked roof and attached arches. Between the vignettes there are sprays of large cabbage roses, dahlias, small flowers and leaves. The upper section of the rim is stippled. On this plate the oriental scene shows a large tall many domed temple at left. A man rides an elephant in the central wooded area and a couple in native costume lounge on the bank in the foreground. A small sail boat is in the river at right.

MADRAS
Made by William Brownfield

 The edge of this dish is decorated with a band of crosses and ovals interspersed at five points by a dark area from which a bouquet of three flowers with dark leaves descends into the rim. Between the floral patterns there is a design of a peony with large, dark, heavily veined leaves and at its right two small temples.

 The central scene shows a large ornate temple at right. It is situated on a riverbank. There is a tall graceful elm at left. A river divides the scene and in the left distance, there are towers and mountains. In the foreground a man stands on the bank and another person kneels beside him. At left, there is a two tiered table surmounted by a large urn. The pattern is printed in lavender.

 Marked W.B., GMK. 660, 1850-71.

MANDARIN
Maker Unknown

The concave rim of this blue printed soup dish is gently lobed at 8 points and the edge is detailed with a band of semi-circles and a curved leaf.

The scene covers the entire plate. The mandarin of the title is seated at center and an attendant with a fan stands near him. Overscaled flowers wreath the central scene. An urn is placed in the wreath at left and a small bird flies above the scene on the upper rim at right.

Marked Opaque China.

"MUSKETEER PATTERN (THE)"

Made by John Rogers and Sons

The indented gadroon edge of this blue and white platter is defined by a dark narrow line set over a row of small white beads. The scene covers the entire dish. Tall dark flowering trees rise from the right foreground and from the left background. The branches meet and frame the scenic picture at the top.

A man wearing a turban and robe rides on his horse in the foreground. He is holding a spear or a musket. He is followed by a gun bearing man and a child on foot. Both men carry round shields on their backs. There is an open air temple in the center of the scene and there are small figures nearby at the end of a long stone wall that extends to the left side of the dish. Four other figures in white are on a large stone stairway which slants upward and presumably leads to the ruins of a temple set high on a hill in the background.

Marked (imp.) Rogers, GMK. 3369, 1814-36. (This pattern name was given by Coysh. For detailed information about the scene see Coysh Dictionary page 255).

NANKIN

Made by Thomas Dimmock

The edge of this plate is slightly indented at twelve places. A narrow band of fretwork and small flowers encircles the upper rim. A bold geometric triangular design consisting of stylized flowers, dark triangular spade shapes and snail-like scrolls separates the scenic reserves in the border pattern. Two opposite reserves show a small boat carrying three persons. A pennant flies from its stern and one of the passengers carries a fringed parasol. The other pair of scenes presents a pavilion with a tall tower at right, a large willow tree at left and some rock forms in the foreground.

A band of brocade frames the central scene of a fenced terrace at left on which a man, woman and child in exotic costumes stand beneath a large parasol held by the man. At right there is a hexagonal garden house with fancy roof which is placed on a rocky island. In the distance there is a boat on a river and on the opposite bank there are a pagoda, some houses and trees.

Marked D, and "Stoneware", GMK. 1297, 1828-59.

ORIENTAL

Maker Unknown

The collar of the pitcher photographed carries a design of eight horizontal bars. Large fruits are placed over the bars and alternate with large flowers. The motifs are separated by a vertical Gothic band of hearts and trefoils framed in diamonds.

A man rides a camel in the center of the scene. A guide holding a pole stands beside him. There is an Asiatic temple at right and a large squat round jar on a pedestal at left. In the background there is a lake and in the distance one sees a temple and towers set against tall mountain peaks. The usual tall elms on either side of the scene frame the picture and there is part of some stone fencing in the foreground.

ORIENTAL BEAUTIES
Mark not located

The white slightly scalloped gadroon edge of this dish is enhanced by a dark band of foliated scrolls and flowerets on the upper part of the concave rim. Pairs of passion flowers alternate with pairs of dahlias around the lower rim. A wreath of small pointed scallops inset with sprigs contains the rim pattern.

The central scene is dominated by a tall vase filled with overscaled flowers at the left. A similar large scroll and flowering tree are at right. Two small human figures stand on a bank in the right foreground. An arched bridge crosses a stream near them. Across the river in the middle distance there is a pavilion on an island and a boat is drawn up to the shore near the structure. There are small buildings and mountains and islands in the background.

Marked Jones.

ORIENTAL BEAUTIES (cont.)

"ORIENTAL FLOWER TREE"

Made by John and William Ridgway

This pattern resembles the famous Indian Tree design. The gadroon edge of the cake plate was left white. A narrow band of small square arches enhances the scalloped gadrooning. Three peony sprays alternate with three small blossoms around the rim. In the center, a tree with overscaled peonies and flowerets rises from some rocks. The divided trunk of the tree forms a "V" under a rock form which is placed across the base of the tree. Marked J. & W.R., Like GMK. 3264, c. 1814-30.

ORIENTAL VASE
Made by Knight, Elkin & Co.

The outer edge of this dish is decorated with a band of beads. The rim is covered with flowers, leaves and curled fern fronds. Four pairs of white fan-like motifs that resemble petals or plumes with a black area framing them at top, are placed around the lower half of the rim.

The flower filled vase of the title is set upon a scroll based pedestal at left. The bouquet it holds stretches across the top of the scene. Flowers in the foreground extend from the pedestal to the right. Two small standing figures are in the lower middle of the scene. Behind them one sees a stream with a sampan. In the distance there are triple roofed pagodas or temples. At the right large scrolls and flowers balance the dominant vase and rise to form a circular picture.

Marked K.E. & Co., GMK. 2301, c. 1826-46.

PALESTINE
(SHECKEM AND SIDON)
Probably made by Elijah Jones

The rims of these plates are lobed in eight places, covered with a stippled ground inset with exotic lily-like flowers, sprays and buds. The blossoms are separated by triangles composed of foliated scrolls. The outer edge is enwreathed with a band of small square crosses on a white ground set over a dark zig-zag line. A wide band of flowerets and lacey trellis crosses the cavetto and is contained by a dark scalloped bank from which a wreath of vertical sprays invades the well.

In the central scene on the Sheckem plate a man on a camel is at right in front of a palm tree. Another man in a robe and turban walks towards a woman seated on a rock at center. There is a jug near her and a covered well gushes water nearby at left. In the background one sees oriental city buildings. Sheckem was a town in ancient Palestine near the city of Samaria (it is now in northwest Jordan; the modern name is Nablus). It was the first capital of the northern kingdom of Israel.

The smaller plate, Sidon, shows a river. In the foreground a man rides a camel or dromedary and another man on foot points to the right. There is a palm tree at left. Across the river spanned by an arched bridge one sees the buildings of a large city. Sidon (Today Saida in Lebanon) was the most ancient city of Phoencia. It was an important port and commercial center. It was known all over the world for purple dyes and glassware. It founded the city of Tyre. These cities were in the northern division of Palestine.

Marked E.J., GMK. 2214, 1831-39.

113

PALESTINE (cont.)

PALESTINE (cont.)

PALESTINE

Made by Ralph Stevenson

The edges of these dark blue plates are gently scalloped and are detailed with a row of tiny straight white lines set over a band of white edged quatrefoils. The scene on the larger plate covers the entire dish. The rim is covered with a floral pattern of small star-shaped flowers. Willow branches fall over the top center of the oriental scene. A temple is at right, a pagoda in the center and in the background there are mountains and trees. There are four figures in the foreground on the larger plate, two are seated, two stand at either side. The man at left smokes a long pipe. The figures on the right wear big fur hats. They appear to be on a rocky bank and a small waterfall spills across the rim at left. The cup plate shows a temple in the background and two small figures with fur hats are placed in the right foreground, one stands, and the other is seated on a boulder.

Marked R. Stevenson, GMK. 3704, c. 1810-32.

PALESTINE (cont.)

PEACOCK

Maker Unknown

The edge of this brown and white dish is outlined by a band of triple scallops that form arches over small triangles. A design of a half-flower is set in the upper section of the border. A row of fringe contains the border design at mid rim.

An oriental personage sits in an elaborate curved chair at right. He holds a baton and points toward the large peacock of the title which spreads its tail across the foreground. Another man stands at center and in the background there are parts of a fence, some exotic plants and willow trees.

Marked 745.

PENANG

Made by Ridgway, Sparks and Ridgway

The outer edge of the soup plate shown is detailed with a stringing band of small rectangles. The background of the circles on the upper part of the rim is covered with narrow concentric lines inset with dark crosses. The same dark linear design appears in the triangular pennants at the bottom of the border. The middle area is filled with white reserves which contain a scroll and bead design.

A mandarin sits in a box enclosure in the center of the scene. He is fishing. Nearby a crane sits on a post of a railing and holds a fish in his beak. At left there is a tall pedestal supporting overscaled prunus blossoms that arch over the scene. At right there is an urn and a large newel post. In the background across some water there is a smaller pavilion.

Marked (imp.) *RSR* and also (imp.) *Staffordshire Knot, GMK. 3299A, c. 1873-79.*

119

PERSIAN

Made by Joseph Heath & Co.

The upper part of the concave rim of this scalloped edge dish is very dark brown. The rest of the border pattern consists of foliated scrolls that resemble cornucopias and flowers. The three largest flowers are a dahlia-type and have a crown-like center. There are shadowy sprigs and buds on the rest of the rim and on the cavetto.

The center design displays a temple made up of three arched sections. The middle part is higher than the others and is crowned with a dome and a tall multilayered spire. The building appears to be Gothic and the entrance arch is topped with a fleur-de-lis. Two small figures wearing turbans and dark cloaks peer out from the porch of the left section, and in the left background there are other buildings. Overscaled flowers fill the foreground.

Marked J.H. & Co. and (imp.) a beaded circle containing a three bladed propeller, GMK. 1994A, 1828-41.

SUSA

Made by Charles Meigh and Son

This dish is twelve sided and the rim is panelled. On the border there are five cartouches containing a scene of Moorish temples and minarets. The reserves are separated by a pennant and scroll design. A band of triple honeycomb covers the cavetto.

Three small figures are placed on a carpeted terrace in the foreground. At right there are steps. There are balustrades at both right and left from the terrace. A river divides the scene vertically. At left in the middle distance one sees the tower and rounded roof of a castle. Behind the castle there are tall mountains. The distinguishing feature of this scene is the very large banana-like plants that appear on either side of the foreground scene.

Marked C.M. & S. and (imp.) "Improved Stone China", It is like GMK. 2620, c. 1851-61.

TEMPLE

Made by Podmore, Walker & Co.

The rim of this plate is concave and is panelled. Foliated scrolls twine around a rope band at the outer edge. In the border there are four shield shapes. Set in the reserves formed by these shapes there are scenes of an oriental temple with two small figures on its steps; large peonies flank the building.

A band of scrolls set in half ovals and a palmetto set in a triangular frame form a wide brocade band around the center scene which is dominated by the large two-handled urn in the left foreground. A stylized temple is at the end of a fence extending from the vase. A small figure with parasol is on the temple steps at the center of the scene. There are rock forms at left that support another temple, a boat on the water in the background and small buildings in the distance. Rock forms in the foreground and part of a fence at left complete the picture. This dish is printed in purple. The pattern is famous in Flow Blue.

Marked P.W. and Co., GMK. 3080, c. 1850.

Scenic Category

ABBEY

Made by Francis Dillon

This saucer is printed in light purple. The border design consists of oval reserves. Framed by foliated scrolls, each oval containing the same picture of a standing man, clad in doublet, pantaloons and boots. He holds a long pole and a large bird is perched at the tip. At right there is a pedestal surmounted with a large urn. The vignettes are separated by floral bouquets, set in angular frames decorated with acanthus leaves. The outer edge of the dish is encircled with a band of quatrefoils and dark spearpoint.

A circle of delicate spearpoint and pendants frame the central scene. The Abbey of the title is in the background and a tall elm rises at left. A man and lady clothed in medieval costume are in the foreground on the bank of a stream that crosses the scene horizontally. In the distance at right there are towered buildings. Clouds complete the circular picture. Marked (ptd.) F.D., and (imp.) Dillon, GMKs. 1288 1N3 1288A, 1834-43.

ALBANO

Probably made by Joseph Heath

The border pattern appears around the collar of the sugar bowl shown and consists of horizontal concentric lines that step up and down in a vertical pattern so that they appear to form horizontal arches. A band of dark scallops controls the design at the bottom, and in turn is followed by a row of bold fleur-de-lis.

In the center scene a man and woman in court dress are on a terrace in the foreground. A wide river divides the scene. At left in the background there is a group of towered buildings and a Roman style temple. A small sailboat is on the river at the left and a bridge crosses the stream in the center background. Tall elms rise at the extreme right.

Albano is in the Alban hills in Italy. It is 15 miles southeast of Rome and located there is Castle Gondolfo, built in the 17th century, the summer residence of the Pope.

Marked J.H. Probably Joseph Heath, GMK. 1993, 1845-53.

ALBION

Possibly made by Ridgway and Morley

The plate and cup plate photographed have seaweed borders with shell-like reserves. The reserves contain a scene of a woman and a child in the foreground and a curving elm at left.

The same center scene appears on both plates photographed. A standing man propels a small open boat carrying two passengers. One holds the tiller, the other one holds nets that seem to contain cork. There is a wooden house and tall trees on the right bank. Tall oaks appear on the left bank. There are towers and town buildings in the distance and two small sailboats are in the background.

The mark is not clear; only the letter "M" is visible. Looks like GMK. 3257. Marked Stoneware, 1842-44.

ALHAMBRA
Maker Unknown

The upper rim of this dish is decorated with pairs of large flowers that alternate with a large peony and buds. The floral designs are linked by ivy vines and leaves at the upper rim. The lower rim is covered with a net. The well is encircled by a band of large and small diamonds. The castle in the center is constructed with many towers. The building is Gothic and is not Arabic. The doorway steps lead down to the waters of a river. At left there are tall elm trees and the bank in the foreground is strewn with small flowers. This printing is in light brown.

ALPINE

Made by William Ridgway

The rim of this white edged saucer is decorated with three oval reserves containing a picture of an urn filled with flowers; these alternate with three shield shaped reserves containing a large open rose. The stippled background is covered with a diaper pattern of arches which resemble modern warheads, each containing a small white star. The rim design covers the cavetto and enters the well.

A very large urn filled with flowers and leaves is set on a plinth on a terrace at left center. The vase has two large handles that are fashioned with masks at the base, and it is decorated on the body with three classic human figures. At right two swans swim in a river and across the water behind a grassy island one sees a mansion or church with towers and a dome. In the distance there are trees and a pointed mountain peak. Clouds complete the circular picture.

The waste bowl has the same pattern inside, but on the outside (shown) the vignette with the urn also contains a picture of the river, the swan, and the towered building.

Marked W.R. and "Opaque China", GMK. 3301, c. 1830-4.

ALPINE (cont.)

ANCIENT ROME

Maker Unknown

The edge of this blue and white dish is lobed in eight places. The border design consists of three mauresque arches filled with small garden flowers. Between each arch there is a large wild rose flanked by foliated scrolls and crowned with triple curves that enclose a stylized rosette. The background on the upper rim consists of two different diaper patterns; one is of hexagonal cells and the other fleur-de-lis. The rim pattern covers the cavetto and is restrained in the well by a band of small white feathery scrolls set over a plain narrow white band.

The central scene is dominated by the tall arch in the background which frames the scene of hills and farmhouses. Tall columns and arches fill the left side of the picture. In the center a group of four people surround the basin of a fountain which is filled from the masked spout at the foot of a statue of a goddess whose arms have been destroyed. Weeds and flowers are encroaching on all the ruins.

ANCIENT ROME (cont.)

ANCONA

Made by Edward and George Phillips

The edge of this unevenly scalloped dish is detailed with a band of small dashes and tiny quatrefoils. The stippled rim is covered with a design of three pairs of large roses and chrysanthemums with very dark leaves which are separated by pale urns and light scrolls crowned with a single open rose. The design enters the cavetto and is contained by a wreath of square pillows centered with quatrefoils. Small beads and spearpoint enter the well below the wreath of square shapes.

A large ornate urn is in the right foreground of the central picture. At left a man is seated near a standing boy. In the distance and across a river there are town buildings and towers. There are tall trees at right behind the urn and tall bamboo trees at left; steps and over-scaled flowers in the foreground complete the scene. (Ancona is an Italian city on the Adriatic, 130 miles northeast of Rome. It was founded in the fourth century B.C. by Greek refugees from Syracuse.) This plate is printed in red and white. Marked E. & G.P., GMK. 3008A, 1822-34.

ANCONA (cont.)

ANTIQUE SUBJECTS
Maker Unknown

The rim of this unevenly scalloped plate is covered with a pattern of diamond shapes containing white quatrefoils which are contained at the edge with a dark band. A wreath consisting of a chain which connects alternating designs of vegetables (radishes and tomatoes) and flowers (a large cabbage rose and a wild rose) is placed around the bottom of the rim. A row of sprigs surrounds the central scene which depicts several figures in a meadow near some water in the foreground. Two persons are astride horses, one steed is white, the other black. A man holds a large dog on a leash at right. In the background there are mountains. A tall elm rises behind the figures at left center.

ATHENS

Probably made by John Rogers and Son

This plate is unevenly scalloped and its white embossed edge is defined by a band of small beads placed over a dark field on the upper rim. A wreath of foliated scrolls and small six-petalled rosettes set in dark circles and scrolls decorated with eight fleur-de-lis pendants encircles the upper rim, and are interspersed with three dark triangular reserves filled with a peony-type flower with leaves, small blossoms and sprigs. In the wide arches between the triangular motifs there are single large roses with two buds, very dark leaves and a spray of five small flowers and leaves at the right. Parts of the three large flowers cross the cavetto and enter the well.

The central scene shows the tall facade of a ruin at left which was the entrance to a temple. Steps lead from the portico down to the river that divides the scene. Three men in a flat boat are near the steps. An arched bridge crosses the stream at center and connects the temple grounds with tall trees on the right bank. There are over-scaled flowers in the foreground.

Marked (imp.) Rogers, GMK. 3369, c. 1814-36.

BARONIAL CASTLES
(Lynden Castle)
Made by John Ridgway and Co.

The edge of this twelve sided plate is decorated with a band of small white acanthus leaves. The rim is covered with a woven pattern of small squares and oblongs. A wreath of scrolls interspersed with a pattern of wild roses with dark leaves alternating with fleur-de-lis is placed over the textured background. A band of spearpoint contains the rim pattern in the cavetto.

In the center the large castle of the title is seen in the background. A river divides the scene and a tall elm rises from the bank at right. There are trees and bushes on the sloping bank across the water at left.

Marked J. Ridgway and Co., GMK. 3259A, pattern registered 1852.

BLUE ITALIAN
Made by Spode

This plate is lobed in eight places on the edge and the concave rim is covered with an Imari pattern according to Robert Copeland. It consists of varied stylized flowers: lotus, chrysanthemum and daisies against various backgrounds of snail diaper, stippled ground and vertical lines. These are set in a wave-like setting on the upper part of the rim. In the curved reserves formed by this on the lower rim there are black sprigs and flowers. The stippled ground covers the cavetto and is contained by a narrow white scalloped line finished with a narrow plain circle.

The central scene covers the well of the dish. A river divides the picture. There is a large ruin of an arch on the far bank in the left foreground and in the background there are towers and trees. In the foreground a woman kneels and a man stands beside her and guides cattle into the stream. A little white lamb is behind them at right. In the right middle distance a girl in a white dress sits in a recess formed by some rocks. There is a stylized elm tree at right.

Marked (imp.) Spode, 27, GMK. 3648, c. 1820-30.

BLUE ITALIAN

Made by Joseph Stubbs

The pattern as it appears on this cup plate eliminates the man and the woman. It shows one cow returning from the stream and the lamb is standing and looking at it. There is no woman in the cave. There is no border pattern as such, just a row of beads.

Marked (imp.) Stubbs, GMK. 3728, 1822-35.

BLUE ITALIAN
Made by Wood and Challinor

This is the same pattern as the one made by Spode. It shows a man and a woman kneeling who are leading some cattle to water in the stream. A woman in white is reading a book as she sits on a square white stone on a white blanket in a cave portion on the right in the middle ground.

Marked W. & C., 1828-43, GMK. 4244.

BOSTON

Made by Charles Meigh

The border pattern appears at the top edge of the pitcher shown and consists of leaves set over a dark band. The scenic transfer on the body presents a group of people who are standing on the bank of a river in the left foreground. A circular stone from a broken column is near them. At left there is a temple ruin. Tall slender trees rise at the center of the scene. A tower and buildings are seen in the background. In the distance across the water there are mountain peaks.

Marked C.M., GMK. 2641A, 1835-49.

BOSTON (cont.)

BOWER

Maker unknown

This light blue dish (10½) is fourteen sided and the panelled rim is covered with reserves containing floral sprays which alternate with shorter geometric designs centered with a diamond. Both patterns are placed over vertical bars, and they are separated by narrow bands of diamonds surmounted by stylized flowers. The outer stippled edge is decorated with a row of tiny diamonds. The border design is contained in the cavetto by a vine of sprigs and posies.

In the central scene, a man and woman dressed in oriental garb stand under the floral and trellis arch that forms the roof of the bower of the title. They are placed on a small circular grassy area framed by a marble bench. There is an urn on a pedestal at left and another pedestal and a pine tree are at right. In the foreground there is a garden chair, and a lute and some music sheets are on the ground. In the background there is a river and in the distance there are buildings, towers and mountain peaks.

"BRITISH COUNTRYSIDE"

Probably made by Enoch Wood & Sons

This cup plate has a henna red edge. The central scene is printed in black and is framed by an octagon. It presents a picture of a stream or lake with large rocks and windswept trees at right with a house on a hill in the background. There are many dark trees in the distance and stippled clouds in the sky.

Marked (imp.) Wood and "N". GMK. 4247, 1818-46.

BRITISH RIVERS
Made by the Clyde Pottery

The edges of these twelve sided plates are outlined by a band of beads. The upper part of the concave rims are stippled. The stippling continues into four oval aprons that descend into the cavetto and are decorated with a bouquet consisting of a pair of large flowers surrounded by small blossoms and leaves. The areas between the stippled patterns are framed with wreaths of hexagons made of rosette beads centered with a narrow white oblong. The same wreaths are placed under the stippled pattern and form a garland punctuated with rosettes around the well.

The scenes differ on the dishes. One plate shown has the river dividing the scene vertically and a tall stylized elm rises from the right flower covered bank. There are castles in the left background. A pair of cows are on the bank in the foreground. The other dish shows the river flowing behind three people, a man, a woman and a child who stand in the foreground. The same type of stylized elm is at left center. A castle is in the right background and is connected to the left bank by a long gently curved rustic bridge.

Coysh states that shards of this pattern have been found marked A.M. for Andrew Muir of the Clyde Pottery at Greenock in Scotland.

Marked C.P. Co., GMK. 935, c. 1850-51.

BRITISH RIVERS (cont.)

BRITISH SCENERY

Made by Davenport

The border design for this pattern is placed around the collar of the pitcher photographed. It consists of grapes, grape leaves and wheat heads contained at the top by a wreath of bell flowers. The scene on the body of the vessel shows cattle in the foreground. They are on the bank of a pond. There is a large stone house across the water and tall elms rise on either side of the scene. The saucer shown has a small rustic cottage in the center.

Marked (imp.) as above, GMK. 1179A, 1805-80.

BRITISH SCENERY (cont.)

BYRON VIEWS SERIES

Made by Copeland and Garrett

In Book I on page 418 a cup plate was catalogued in this pattern and given the name "Sicily" in order to list it. It bore no name on the back-stamp. Here is a different cup plate that has no title on the reverse.

Marked as above and "Late Spode", G.M.K. 1092, c. 1833-47.

148

CASTLE PATTERN

Made by Baker, Bevans & Irwin

The border design on this plate covers the cavetto and is contained by a white dentil around the central scene. The design on a stippled ground contains three oriental floral motifs that contain a fish-like shape at the base and which alternate with a heraldic theme of fleur-de-lis on a dark background.

In the central picture the gate of Sebastian is shown at left. There is a pair of stylized trees set on a rocky bank at right. A stream divides the scene. It is spanned by a two-arched bridge that extends from the gate structure. A pair of swans float in the right foreground. There are several figures in the picture, two are on the road that passes under the gate, two others are seated on a large flat rock at extreme left. A herdsman and three cows are in the foreground and there are three men on the arched bridge.

This is the same pattern that was made by Spode (see Coysh I page 76).

Marked (imp.) as above and printed B.B. & I. and "Opaque China", Glamorgan Pottery Swansea, Wales 1813-38, GMKs. 226,227.

149

"CASTLE TOWARD"
Made by John Hall & Sons

This deep little (5½") dish is printed in cobalt. The narrow outer band is decorated with a flame motif. The border design consists of large flowers, peonies and Sweet Williams separated by fruit, peaches and grapes.

The central scene of a castle on a hill overlooking a stream is framed by narrow white lace.

Coysh states that the castle is in Argylshire, and that it was built by David Hamilton in 1821 for a wealthy merchant, Kirkham Finley, who became Lord Provost of Glasgow.

Marked J. Hall & Sons, GMK. 1887, 1822-32.

CASTLE TOWARD (cont.)

CETARA
Bay of Salerno
(Series 106)

One of the designs from this series is shown in Book I on page 351 *(Oberwessel on Rhine) and in this book we also list Venice, Series 106. The plates in this series are deeply scalloped and the outer edges are detailed with a band of dark beads. The rims are decorated with a spray of white ferns that alternate with bell flowers and bouquets of roses and sprigs. The bottom of the rims are encircled by a twisted rope design interspersed with fleurons. The rim of the cup plate is identical to the large dishes but the rope around the well is eliminated. The central scene on this plate has a tower at right and sailboats at left and a small oar-propelled boat with two persons in the center foreground. There are city towers in the background and mountains in the distance.*

Marked E. Wood & Sons, GMK. 4261, 1818-46.

152

CINTRA

Probably made by Joseph Heath

The concave rim of this twelve sided plate is covered with a pattern of wavy bands set over a background of narrow concentric lines. The design resembles moiré. A narrow wreath of cartridge scrolls is placed around the outer edge and the bottom of the border pattern is contained in the cavetto by a band of small scallops set upon a wreath of Greek keys and fleur-de-lis.

In the center scene a man holding a pole walks beside a woman who sits side-saddle on a donkey. A small boy is on the right side of the donkey. They are on a road at right which is contained by a flat stone wall at left. Behind the wall at left there is a large house with a tiled roof. There are tall elms and some bushes and part of a statue at right. There are towered buildings and mountain peaks in the left background. Cintra is in Portugal.

Marked J.H., mark not located, 1845-53.

153

CIRCASSIA

Possibly made by Samuel and James Boyle

This plate is fourteen sided and the edge of the concave rim is outlined with small snail scrolls. The rim is covered with a pattern of swirling oak leaves and berries which is contained at the cavetto with a scalloped circle of narrow fringe. The central river scene on this plate is dominated by the arched bridge in the center. It connects a temple with columns in the right background to the left bank where a tall elm tree rises. In the foreground there are three small figures on the sharp bank at center.

Marked S.J. & J.B., could be GMK. 734, c. 1842-3.

CLARA

Made by John Ridgway

The border decoration on this scalloped dish is composed of pairs of flowing feather-like scrolls that alternate with trios of small roses, leaves and sprigs. Both designs are set upon a ribbon band that encircles the middle of the rim. The border pattern is contained at the bottom by a band of small pointed arches. There is a boat in the foreground of the central scene which is divided by a river. A man stands in the vessel and points to the left shore. Another man seated in the stern pulls an oar in the water. Two women are seated in the prow. At the right there is a stone landing with stairs and railings and a pair of large square posts. Tall elms rise behind the landing platform. At left in the background there is a Greek temple with towers and in the distance an arched bridge crosses the stream.

Marked J.R. and Stoneware, GMK. 3257, c. 1830-41.

CLEOPATRA

Maker Unknown

This twelve sided plate has a slightly concave rim which is decorated with a design of five large open dahlias interspersed between scrolled cartouche that contain round fruits: melons, cherries and a few grapes. The upper part of the rim is covered with a cellular diaper pattern. The points of the scrolls beneath the floral and fruit design enter the well.

In the center scene in the left middle ground there are ruins of Egyptian temples and an obelisk. A pyramid can be seen very faintly in the middle distance. There is a balustrade ending in a pedestal topped with an urn in the center foreground. An overscaled ruffled flower and a tall flowering tree dominate the right foreground. This pattern is printed in a purple transfer decorated with yellow and green. It was also made in flow blue.

COLOGNE

Made by Elkin, Knight & Bridgwood

The edge of this mulberry printed saucer is encircled by a band of ovals and rosettes which is interrupted at eight points by six-petalled flowers set upon a dark triangle with pendent base. Various realistic flowers are placed around the rim and are connected by garlands just above the well.

An ornate church and tower is in the left middle ground of the central scene. It is surrounded by tall lacy trees. A sail boat with upturned prow, holding three men is on the river that flows from the foreground to the right background. A clump of bushes is at right. There are other buildings in the right background, and pointed mountains in the distance. Flowers are strewn across the foreground.

Marked EK&B, GMK. 1464, 1827-40.

COMBUSNDHAM ON THE CLYDE
Made by Belle Vue Pottery

This plate is gently scalloped and the outer edge is decorated with a row of light beads on a dark ground interrupted by twelve small shield forms with dark centers. The upper part of the rim is stippled and small flowering branches are placed between the shields on the stippled ground. Three large peonies flanked by very dark leaves and smaller blossoms alternate around the lower rim and enter the well with sprays of small flowers and sprigs. sprigs.

In the center a Gothic country house is seen in the background. It has towers at its corners and eight tall spires on its roof at right. It sits in its park behind a lacey fence that crosses the scene. A man with a high hat and a lady with parasol stand at an opening at the fence at left. In the right foreground three cows graze near a tall slender tree. A pair of the same trees can be seen at the far left behind the fence. Another example in this series is named "Carstairs on the Clyde" and it is pictured in Book I on page 219.

Marked Belle Vue, GMK. 322, c. 1826-41.

CONTINENTAL VIEWS
(Mt. Olympus)
Made by Machin & Potts

The concave panelled rim of this unevenly scalloped dish is covered with circular sprigs and stylized flowers with six jagged petals that resemble pinwheels. The border design covers the cavetto and is contained in the well by a wreath of small beaded scallops interspersed with rosettes.

The central scene is dominated by the very high double-arched viaduct in the center background. Four people in native costume are near some small rocks at left. Two men are seated and one holds a staff. Two women stand nearby and one is playing a mandolin. There are very dark, tall trees rising at left and a dark shrub-covered bank at right. In the background there are town buildings, towers and a belfry. In the distance a sloping meadow leads to a high triangular mountain.

Mark M. & P., mark not located. See Godden, page 404, 1833-7. See Soracte.

CONTINENTAL VIEWS
(Soracte)
Made by Machin & Potts

This is the same pattern as Mt. Olympus. It does not differ in any detail at all. Soracte is in Etruria, which is a district north of Rome.

Marked as above. Also marked Patent, also M. & P., GMK. 2456A, 1833-37.

COTTAGE

Maker Unknown

The collar of this cream pitcher is decorated with part of the border pattern that appears on dishes. The outer edge is detailed with a band of triangular lines and small white beads. Part of large flowers and leaves can be seen against the diaper background of diamonds centered with beads. There are probably scenic reserves between the flowers.

The cottage of the title is a Swiss type. It is at right and has a balcony set over dark twisted pillars that form a porch below. A very tall epi rises from the fancy slanted roof over the balcony. At far right one can see a multi-paned bay window and a wide white house section and four tall chimneys. At left (not visible in this picture) there is a small wooden cabin with thatched roof. A large lake, pond and Alpine mountains are in the distance. There are large flowers strewn across the foreground.

"COUNTRY MANOR"

Mady by Enoch Wood & Sons

   This cup plate is printed in medium blue and the gently indented edge is defined by a rope border. The scene covers the entire dish including the indented rim. A large house is in the left center, it is flanked by big bushes and tall trees. A man dressed in white reclines on the ground in the right foreground. There is water in the foreground, a tall elm rises at right. Clouds above complete the circular picture.

CRYSTAL PALACE

Made by J. & M. P. Bell & Company

This blue and white platter has a border design consisting of scroll-framed vignettes set in a background of vertical bars filled with narrow concentric lines. Each of the reserves contains a picture of a famous English building, the one at the top of the dish shows Windsor Castle. A narrow band of beaded scallops and dots contains the border design at the well.

The central scene features the Crystal Palace the site of the great Exhibition of 1851. In the foreground there are groups of people in Victorian dress, and pairs of equestrians. A tall elm rises in the middle ground and other elms are at extreme right and left.

Marked J. & M. P. Bell & Co., and a figure of Brittania. GMK. 318, c. 1850-70.

DACCA

Made by Minton and Boyle

The dishes photographed are unevenly scalloped and the edges are defined with white beads. The rim is stippled and the upper third is very dark and the lower section is light. A wreath of foliated scrolls and fleur-de-lis separates the shades. A wreath of flowers and sprigs is set in the light section and enters the cavetto which is covered with a wide band of narrow vertical lines contained at the well by a wreath of bay leaves and berries.

The plate presents a suburban scene. A man rides a horse on a roadway in front of a villa and a round tower surrounded by stone walls. There are other people on foot on the road. A villa and square tower are at left on a hillside. A large body of water is in the middle ground. In the distance there are other buildings and mountain peaks.

The scene on the platter is bucolic. Cattle are grazing in the foreground and there is a lake or waterway at left. There are tall elms on the left bank in the foreground and several flat stones are scattered across the scene. At right there are tall Gothic ruins of towered buildings and arches. Dacca is a city in Palestine.

The plate photographed is printed in sepia. The platter is printed in light green.

Marked M. & B., GMK. 2693, c. 1836-41.

DACCA (cont.)

DAVENPORT II

Made by Davenport

The edge of this unevenly scalloped plate is white. A line of dark beads follows the pattern of the edge and separates the white outer border from the rim pattern which extends to the central circular scene. The border design consists of berry forms decorated with single flowers and white leaves and dark shadowy snowflakes centered with white rosettes.

A narrow lacey frame that contains fleur-de-lis surrounds the central scene. A river is in the center; there are tall elms on either bank, and a tower and adjacent buildings on the right bank. A man and boy stand on the left bank in the foreground. In the distance there are mountains. The rim of the cup plate carries a single row of the border design. The scene in the center is slightly different from the larger plate and the human figures have been omitted.

Marked as above. GMK. 1181A, 1820-60.

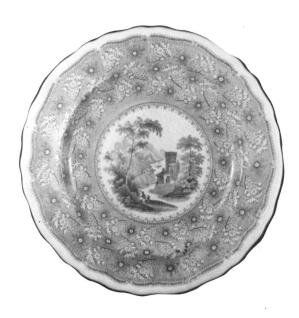

DAVENPORT II (cont.)

DAVENPORT III

Made by Davenport

    The scalloped edge of this dish is embossed and a narrow band of straight thick fringe is placed under the embossed ridge. The plate is printed in light purple. The design on the rim is contained under the fringe by narrow lacey scallops from which small beads are suspended. Five pairs of peonies separate the five reserves which show two small birds with long beaks facing each other as they perch on scrolls. Behind them there are willow trees.

    A wreath of tiny fleur-de-lis and beads surround the central scene of a Gothic church with a cross on its spire which is placed on a river bank in the right middleground. In the foreground, a man dressed in oriental robe and peaked hat stands on the river bank and holds a large jar. Tall elms rise on either side of the scene and there are overscaled flowers in the right foreground.

    Marked as above and with an (imp.) anchor. GMK. 1181, 1805 plus.

DAVENPORT III (cont.)

DORIA

Made by Barrow & Co.

The panelled rim of this ten sided plate is decorated with three scenic reserves framed in foliated scrolls, each showing the same square temple and arch with a very tall curved arch entrance at center. The scenic designs are separated by a triangular scroll that contains a square cross. The background of this area of the border is covered with a diaper pattern of tiny dotted squares. The border pattern is contained in the cavetto by a pointed wreath of elongated fleur-de-lis that gives a fencing effect.

In the center the same temple with arch appears as shown in the border reserves. It is at right. Wide steps lead up to it. Balustrades frame the steps and a grassy terrace in the foreground. A group of four people in court dress stand together on the terrace and a small white dog is nearby. In the distance there is a Tuscan mansion set beneath tall mountain peaks.

Marked (imp.) as above and "Ironstone China", also with an English coat of arms.

Mark not located.

EASTERN SCENERY II

Made by Enoch Wood and Sons

The unevenly scalloped edge of this plate is outlined by a narrow band of beads. The border design consists of lacey net draperies pinned into swags at the top with rosettes. Large blossoms, leaves, wild roses and buds are placed over the lace and descend into the well.

A small open temple is set in the center of the scene. It has turrets and arches that appear to be Gothic but are intended to be Oriental in design. A man and woman stand under an arch at the right. A river divides the scene horizontally. A sailboat is near the temple and there is a castle with a tower on the far bank. Over-scaled leaves and blossoms rise on a tree behind the temple. This transfer was printed with a lavender border and a purple center. (This was listed in Book I on page 704 as "Unknown Scenic 9). The second plate shown is printed in mulberry.

Marked E.W. & S., GMK. 4260, 1818-46.

EASTERN SCENERY II (cont.)

EGINA

Made by Edward Challinor & Co.

This twelve sided plate is printed in mulberry. The concave panelled stippled rim is covered with narrow concentric lines, and a white vine wreath has been placed over the lines. A band of small dentils in the cavetto contains the border pattern.

In the foreground of the center picture three persons and a small dog stand on the banks of a river. In the background at left there is an imposing palace. On the right bank a statue is placed on a pedestal at the foot of two large elms.

Marked E. Challinor & Co., GMK. 836, 1853-60.

EGYPTIAN

Probably made by Joseph Heath

The white edge of this dish is scalloped and a wreath of heavy white scrolls is placed around the upper dark stippled rim. A diaper pattern of small beaded squares covers the lower rim and ends in a band of quatrefoils and a succeeding band of teardrop shapes ending in diamonds.

In the central scene there are temple ruins at right and a sphinx on a pedestal. The Nile divides the scene. At left there is a statue of a seated Pharoah placed under the shade of a tall exotic tree. In the middle background there are pyramids and obelisks.

Laidecker lists this pattern as being in purple and marked J.H. & Co. This example is printed in purple.

Marked J.H. & Co., (according to Laidecker), GMK. 1994A, 1828-41.

"ENGLISH FARM SCENE"

Made by Frances Dillon

The upper stippled rim of this pattern is trimmed with a band of dark beads. Pairs of large roses and dahlias separated by foliated scrolls and bunches of five forget-me-nots are placed around the center of the concave rim. Shadowy sprigs and buds cover the bottom of the border pattern and the cavetto.

A woman and two children stand in front of their cottage in the left middle distance of the picture. Four fat sheep are in the right foreground. Two are eating from their feed rack. The foreground is covered with shrubs and there is a brook at left. Tall trees rise at either side of the scene and there is a mountain peak in the distance. This platter is printed in blue and white.

Marked (imp.) Dillon, GMK. 1288, 1834-43.

FESTOON BORDER

Made by Enoch Wood and Sons

The unevenly scalloped concave rim of this dish is covered with a pattern containing six reserves. Three of the reserves picture different suspension bridges and the other three feature typical Victorian garden follies. They are separated by over-scaled flowers from which floral festoons are suspended and enwreath the central scene.

In the center the scene is dominated by a large Gothic church-like building that features ten very large multi-paned windows. The building is situated on the high bank of a river, pond or a stream, and the windows are reflected in the water. At right a single tall elm rises from the brush covered bank and a small row boat is pulled up behind the tree. In the foreground a rocky bank contains bushes and a group of white flowers or a flock of small white birds.

A small part of the border pattern appears on the cup plate and can be recognized only by the top sections of the suspension bridges. The central scene is the same with the exception that the row boat is not seen. These plates come in many colors and many combinations of colors such as pink and green, purple and aqua, etc.

Marked E. Wood and Sons, GMK. 4261, 1818-46.

FESTOON BORDER (cont.)

FLORENCE

Made by William Adams & Sons

The stippled borders of these dishes are covered with narrow concentric lines. A wreath of mossy sprigs that form scrolls which are covered with small white bubbles is placed around the rim. The outer edge is decorated with a band of oval beads, and the bottom of the border design is contained by a narrow line interspersed with fleur-de-lis.

The central scenes differ in this pattern and on the platter there is a large gondola on a river in the middle of the scene. There are several people in the boat and there are other gondolas in the background. Tall trees rise on either side of the stream and marble steps descend to the water. Large rectangular castle-like buildings and an arched bridge are seen in the background. On the plate there is a small boat being poled by a standing man and two people seated in the boat. There are tall elms on the right bank and across the stream there is a building with a cupulo.

Marked W. Adams and Son and also (imp.) W. Adams and Son in a half circle, GMK. 22, 1819-64.

FLORENCE (cont.)

FLORENCE

Made by John Rogers & Son

This plate is unevenly scalloped and the edge is finished with a band of small narrow white scallops. Four scenic reserves are placed around the rim and each shows the scene of a large domed building at left in the middleground. It is connected to a long bridge which crosses a wide river. In the left foreground a small dark boat is pulled up to shore and at right there are parts of a tall dark arch. The reserves are separated by a diamond diaper design framed with flowers set over a large open blossom with dark leaves crossing the cavetto and entering the well.

In the central picture there is a church-like building with large domed tower in the right middleground. Its pediment is topped with a statue, faces a river. There is a small dark boat afloat in the center of the scene. At left there is a large dark pedestal topped with an urn filled with large flowers. Other overscaled flowers are placed at its base.

Marked (imp.) Rogers, GMK. 3369, 1814-36.

FOUNTAIN
Made by Robert May

The outer white edge of this soup dish carries a dark band of ovals and darts. The upper part of the concave rim is stippled. A design of large open roses and leaves alternating with dahlias are separated by curved chevrons with an oval feathered pendant.

The fountain of the title is in the foreground of the central scene. It is set on a hexagonal base with dolphins supporting the first level and cranes the upper level. This dominates the scene. A man, woman, child and dog stroll nearby. At right a tall curved tree rises from bushes. A river divides the scene and an arched bridge is seen in the background. A tower with a domed top sits high on a hill in the left background. Clouds complete the circular picture. The plate is blue and white.

FOUNTAIN (cont.)

DETAIL

FOUNTAIN SCENERY
Made by Samuel Alcock

The plate showing a deer on the pedestal of a fountain was illustrated in Book I page 265. It is pink and was used for the cover of Book I. That plate was made by William Adams and Sons. This dish was printed in a dark, medium blue that was allowed to flow.

Marked S. Alcock, Hill Pottery, Burslem. GMK. 76, 1830-59.

"GARDEN SCENE"

Made by Knight and Elkin

The scalloped edge of this cup plate is detailed with a white band. The rim design of dark scrolls, small white flowers and larger five-petal blossoms that resemble morning glories is set against a background of vertical dark lines on a stippled ground. The rim pattern covers the cavetto and forms a circle around the central scene.

In the center there is a large dark two-handled urn set on a white dish at left. A wine glass is set next to it. They are placed on a terrace overlooking a lake in which a tall fountain rises from a rocky island. At left in the background there are tall elms. Trees and shrubs and over-scaled flowers and hollyhock-type blossoms are in the right foreground.

Marked (imp.) with an eagle, for mark see Hannibal Passing the Alps in this book, 1826-46.

GEM

Made by William Ridgway

The fourteen sided plate shown is edged with a row of tiny crosses. The rim is covered with a vermicelli (worm track) design decorated with four horizontal groups of three wild white roses which alternate with small dark spiked sprigs and with five small white blossoms. A band of pickets contains the border pattern.

In the central scene on the larger plate a tall elm rises at left. At its base are stone steps flanked by pedestals surmounted with reclining lions. In the central foreground there is a group of four figures. A man and a woman stand conversing with a seated woman and a cavalier with sword and slanted hat, who are resting on a bench. A small dog stands hearby. There is an urn behind the bench. A river divides the scene at right and across the water there is a double roofed pavilion surmounted with an epi. There are sailboats in the center of the picture, and in the distance there are other block buildings and towers.

The cup plate has no trim on its fourteen sided edge. Part of the border design is missing and in the central scene the stone steps appear but the pedestals and lions are omitted and there are only the two seated figures, the cavalier and the lady who are at right. The platter is printed in sepia and the cup plate is lavender.

Marked W.R., GMK. 3301, 1830-34.

185

GENEVESE

Made by Edge Malkin and Co.

The outer dark edge of this pitcher and basin are decorated with small foliated scrolls and flowerettes. The central scene is the same on both pieces and consists of a Swiss chalet with an epi on its slanting roof at left. There is a church across a river and at right tall elms rise from the bank. There are over-scaled flowers placed across the foreground. This transfer is multi-colored over a sepia printed base.

Marked E.M. & Co., GMK. 1445, c. 1873.

GENOA

Made by Robert Cochran & Co.

The border design appears on the slightly concaved rim of this dish. It consists of a background of narrow concentric lines. Five scenic reserves picture a castle in the background connected to the left bank of a river by a high triple-arched bridge. A pair of swans swim in the foreground. The reserves are separated by shields filled with a diamond diaper pattern and flanked by large flowers.

In the central picture a seated woman and three standing men are on the bank of a river in the foreground. The river divides the scene. There is a tall pedestal topped with a large urn and part of a balustrade at right. Tall elms rise behind the balustrade. A castle is in the left background across the river and peaked mountains are in the distance. A small boat is midstream.

Marked R.C. & C., GMK. 965, c. 1846 plus.

187

GOTHIC
Made by Davenport

The rim of this sauce tureen stand is covered with a design of scrolls that form arches. In the arches a pattern composed of a large trefoil flanked by smaller ones and with a bouquet of sprigs pendent toward the center alternates with a similar design composed of five small trefoils from which a small sprig is pendent.

At left in the central scene, divided by a river, there are Gothic buildings with a small watch-tower which extends into the water. A very tall elm rises from a grassy bank at right. There is a sailboat near the building and in the distance one sees other towers and buildings. This is printed in Flow Blue.

Marked Davenport, it is like marked GMK. 1187, 1820-60.

GOTHIC

Made by Thomas Dimmock

The unevenly scalloped outer edge of this dish is decorated with a band of bell flowers and darts. The rim design consists of three cartouches, each containing a large convoluted shell set in a reserve with shadowy flowers, sprigs and seaweed. Three hexagonal patterns containing white stylized flowers separate the shell designs. A band of square arched forms set on angles over sprigs are placed around the cavetto. The central scene contains a picture of the ruins of the Gothic arch of a former church and seen through the arch in the distance is another church building. There are a pair of deer in the foreground, one reclines, the other stands nearby. In the distance across the river there is a large house and tower.

Marked D., GMK. 1297, 1828-59.

189

GOTHIC

Probably made by Jacob Furnival & Co.

This fourteen sided dish (8") is printed in slate blue that has a flown quality. The panelled concave rim displays a border of grapes, grape leaves, tendrils and foliated scrolls. The lower sections of the grape bunches invade the cavetto.

In the central scene a large Gothic structure is at right. A river divides the scene and there are other buildings and a bridge in the background. Tall elms and small pines grow on the left bank and a woman and child stand near one of the pines. There are rocks and shrubs in the foreground and at right there are other rocks and a curving tree.

This pattern was made in cobalt Flow Blue and in a very dark mulberry.

The Flow Blue dishes are marked J.F. & Co., GMK. 1643, 1847-70. (The backstamp photographed is that of an American importer.)

GOTHIC (cont.)

GOTHIC

Made by Thomas Mayer
Also made by Charles Meigh

This pattern is shown on a cup plate in Book I page 712 as an unknown scenic #20 (US20). There is no backstamp on that cup plate. It is shown again here. It bears the border design of pheasants and there is a quatrefoil chain around the central scene.

The second cup plate carries a very bold border design and the central scene covers the well. Note the heavy embossed wave-like edge on this plate. It is marked (imp.) Stone China and Hanley, the mark used by Charles Meigh.

The border on the saucer is the same as on the first cup plate. The saucer is marked by Thomas Mayer. The central scenes are approximately the same on all three dishes. There are minor differences in the background transfers of the bridges and towers.

Three men in a sailboat approach a landing near a tall stone building with steeply sloped roof surmounted on the ridge with an ornate epi. There is a stylized elm behind the building, and mountains in the background. Overscaled flowers fill the foreground.

An example of this pattern is in the Royal Scottish Museum. It is impressed "Dixon", made by the Sunderland Pottery. (See plate 28, page 27 in Sunderland Ware).

Marked (imp.) T. Mayer, Stoke, GMK. 2659, 1828-35. (Marked imp.) Improved Stone China, Hanley, GMK. 2618, 1835-49).

GOTHIC (cont.)

GOTHIC BEAUTIES

Made by Thomas Ingleby & Co.

The unevenly scalloped edge of this plate is white. The background of the upper part of the rim is stippled. A design of six rounded triangular reserves is placed about the upper rim. Each is centered at the top by bold scalloped semi-circles, three of which are trimmed with white petals and the alternate three left plain. Various floral sprays are placed in the arches formed by the lower part of the triangular design.

The central scene, framed by a wreath of tiny snail-like scrolls, depicts a large Gothic church in the center. A woman and a little girl, each wearing a wide brimmed hat, are in the foreground. A tall mimosa tree and other lacey trees are at left. There is a willow at right. In the background there are hills, a river and some towers. Clouds complete the circular scene. (This was listed in Book I, page 716 as "Unknown, Scenic Pattern 28". Note that it has no border design and the edge is enwreathed only by the snail-like scrolls.)

Marked T.I. & Co., GMK. 2140, 1834-35.

GOTHIC TEMPLE

Made by C. & W.K. Harvey

The border of this platter resembles herringbone composed of a verti-cal design of chevrons and diamonds. The top and the bottom of the border are contained by a chain of ovals containing diamonds. A band of small spearpoint is placed around the well.

The central scene is divided by a river. It is dominated by a large Gothic tower at center left with a niche containing the statue of a crowned monarch. A balustrade at left descends to the river from a flower strewn platform. In the foreground two men and two ladies in Edwardian dress are on a grassy bank. There are balustrades and a railing at right and a tall elm rises behind the railing. In the distance there are other Gothic buildings, mountains and clouds.

Marked (imp.) Harvey and Opaque China, GMK. 1967, c. 1835-53. (There is also a printed H in the backstamp.)

GOTHIC TEMPLE (cont.)

GRECIAN FONT II

Made by William Adams and Sons

In Book I a saucer is shown that bears the same title and the maker's mark as appears on this dish. That design is completely different in border pattern and central scene. The shell framed reserves on the border of this plate contain a scene of two men standing in the foreground on the shore of a large body of water. A three-masted boat is in the background, and a tower is on a cliff at right. In the distance there are mountain peaks. The vignettes are separated by a group of shells, seaweeds and pods. The outer edge is detailed by a band of beads.

The central scene is dominated by the tall ornate fountain in the foreground. A peacock is drinking from the basin and another stands on a balustrade framed platform near the base of the fountain. At left there is an arch and a lady and gentleman in court dress are descending steps below the arch. In the background a river divides the scene and on the right bank there is a little house with a small boat pulled up nearby.

Marked W.A. & S., (imp.) Adams, GMK. 23, 1819-64.

GRECIAN FONT II (cont.)

HIBERNIA
Made by John Wedgwood

A wreath of white foliated scrolls surrounds the scalloped edge of the dish shown. The stippled background on the border is covered with a basket weave pattern. A wreath of white berries, grapes, leaves and tendrils is placed around the lower concave rim. The design covers the cavetto and is contained in the well by foliated scrolls and small gooseberries.

An arched bridge crosses a narrow stream in the central scene and a large domed building is at left and some buildings with pillars are in the left background. A street scene can be observed in the right distance.

A small boy sits and fishes on a concrete embankment in the right foreground. Many small boats are tied up near the bridge.

Hibernia is an old name for Ireland. The city may be Dublin and the narrow river, the Liffey.

The border is printed in red with a white wreath; the center scene is in blue.

The red and white cup plate shown has no central picture.

Marked J. Wedgwood, like GMK. 4276B, c. 1841-60.

HIBERNIA (cont.)

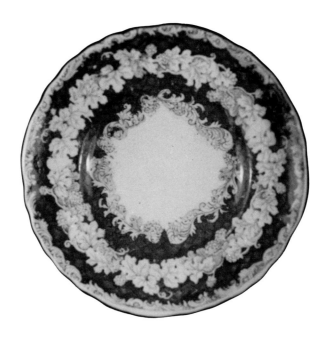

IRISH SCENERY

Made by Elkin, Knight & Elkin

The indented stippled flange of this soup dish is slightly scalloped and is covered with a paisley pattern consisting of bold foliated scrolls, vertical cascades of bell flowers, three fan shapes and three three-leaf clover shapes which alternate around the rim. The stippling of the background covers the cavetto and is contained in the well by a Greek key motif.

In the central scene a man, wearing a hat and short trousers, bearing a backpack, carries a stick and drives a donkey along a path beside a lake or river. At right there is a very large and tall pine tree and some rocks and bushes. A sailboat carries two figures on the water. In the background a three-storied country mansion sits atop the steep bank. Trees are placed on both sides of the building and there is a triangular mountain peak in the distance. It is printed in dark rose.

The second plate printed in mulberry shows a castle set high on a bluff. Marked Elkins & Co., GMK. 1468A, 1822-30.

IRISH SCENERY (cont.)

ISOLA BELLA II
Made by William Adams & Sons

In Book I page 299 a platter and a cup plate are shown entitled "Isola Bella". The teapot illustrated here is also backstamped Isola Bella, but the border design has been changed and consists of star-like medallions flanked by curved sprigs and set against a sprigged background. The central scene consists of column ruins, a garden house, statue, and curved balustrades at the left, a tall elm at right and a couple in court dress in the foreground. Marked W. Adams & Sons, GMK. 228, c. 1819-64.

ISOLA BELLA II (cont.)

LAKE

Made by Ashworth

This pattern was first produced by Frances Morley and Co. in the 1840's as shown in the following description. The Canadian view here was taken from a series by W.H. Bartlett from the same series by W.H. Bartlett and is "Church at Point Levi" (Quebec). The company of Frances Morley and Company joined with Ashworth and became Morley and Ashworth. They produced this pattern also.

The mark shown here, (imp.) Ashworth, is GMK. 137 and dates 1862-80. The Morley mark or the F.M. mark dates 1845-1858. NOTE: Morley and Ashworth dated 1859 to 1862; once their marks were M. & A. This pattern was made in Flow Blue by Frances Morley.

LAKE

Made by Frances Morley & Co.

The border pattern of the slightly indented rims of these dishes has a background of narrow concentric lines. A wreath of white feathery foliated scrolls surrounds the rim and is interspersed with pairs of roses with dark garlands under them, which alternate with garlands suspended by hooks formed by the white scrolls. The concentric lines cover the cavetto and are contained in the well by small snail-like scrolls set under a narrow white band.

The center scene is Canadian and shows an Iroquois Indian encampment. There are teepees at the right on the high bank of a river; an Indian stands near the tent, and another is seated near him. There are canoes in the water. Tall trees rise on all the islands in the background.

The scene is "Scene Among the Thousand Isles" (Canadian View), after an engraving by William Henry Bartlett in CANADIAN SCENERY by N.P. Willis. For the Morley mark, see Larson who notes the letters F.M. on the base of an urn carrying the name of a Philadelphia retailer.

Marked FM. GMK. 2759, 1845-58.

LAKE OF COMO

Probably made by Wood and Challinor

The white scalloped edge of this dish is defined by a band of dark beads centered with white crosses. The transfer print is black. The upper part of the border is filled with white foliated scrolls that separate two different floral groups, one of which contains sunflowers and sprigs, the other roses with sharply defined serrated rose leaves, a wreath of scallops and diamonds gives a spearpoint effect around the well.

In the center picture a tall slender tree rises from the lake bank in the foreground. In the left background there is a lakeside open air pavilion, tall towers and other buildings. A many covered pleasure boats are on the water and one sees mountains in the distance.

Marked W.&C. GMK. 4244, 1828-43.

LAKE SCENERY
Made by Enoch Wood & Sons

This pitcher is printed in a raspberry pink. Large foliated white scrolls are placed over a stippled ground under the lip. The same scrolls, with the addition of twining vines over triple bars, frame the nine different vignettes on the collar and inside the lip. There are different lake views on either side of the vessel. The base is encircled by the vine trimmed band.

Marked E.W.&S. GMK. 4260, 1818-46.

LAKE SCENERY (cont.)

LAKE SCENERY (cont.)

LANDSCAPE

Made by Wedgwood

The large plate that shows the temple ruin on the high bank at left is a recent re-issue of a pattern made earlier. The two smaller dishes are older and are impressed with a date letter for 1878. All bear the distinctive border of large open cabbage roses alternating with peony-type blossoms set against a stippled ground. The outer edges are detailed with a band of beads strung on a narrow line set under a dark scallop. The two small dishes are rose colored. The larger dish is dark blue and is marked Etruria, England and would date c. 1899.

Marked (imp.) Wedgwood, GMK. 4075, 1860 plus.

LANDSCAPE (cont.)

LANERCOST PRIORY

Made by Minton

The blue dish pictured is a miniature platter (6 inches). The edge is detailed with a dark band of scrolls. The border covers the stippled rim and consists of morning glories and slanted spotted narrow leaves all trailing to the right. The ancient priory of the title is pictured in the center.

Marked (imp.) Mintons, GMK. 2706. Godden states Mintons (with the "s") dates after 1871.

LAODICEA

Made by Charles James Mason and Company

The scalloped white edge of this pale green and white plate is embossed, and a band of small scrolls and darts defines the white area. The border design of ribbon enclosed reserves contain female allegorical figures alternating with floral reserves topped with ewers and jugs. It is the same border pattern used by Mason on his Napoleon series.

The central scene is a desert encampment of Arabian tents. There are Arab men and women seated near tall palm trees.

This same scene, with a border design of large acanthus leaves was used by Scott's Southwick Pottery (Sunderland) and titled "Arabia" (1866).

Laodicea was an ancient Phoenician city which prospered under the Romans (The Latin name was Laodicea ad Mare [Laodicea on the sea]. It is is located in Syria on the Mediterranean and is opposite Cyprus, 110 miles north of Beirut. Its modern name is Latakia.

Marked C.J.M. & Co., GMK. 2532, 1829-45.

LAODICEA (cont.)

IN THE EARLY AGE OF CHRISTIANI-
-TY, LAODICEA WAS BLESSED WITH
A FLOURISHING CHURCH, AS St PAULS
EPISTLE TO THE COLOSSIANS AT-
TEST.(*ll.1. IV. 16*). NOT A SINGLE CHRIS-
-TIAN NOW LIVES THERE ITS TEM-
-PLES, ARE DESOLATE AND THE MAG-
-NIFICENT BUILDINGS OF ANCIENT
LAODICEA ARE NOW FREQUENTED BY
WOLVES AND JACKALLS. THE MO-
-HAMMEDANS HAVE A MOSQUE THERE
IN WHICH PRAYERS ARE DAILY HEARD.

C. J. M & Co

LAWRENCE

Mark not located

The background of the concave panelled rim of this twelve sided plate is covered with narrow concentric lines. Five scenic reserves are set against this background. Each shows a banister and balustrade at right and two figures stand next to it. At left there are willows and in the background are towers.

These reserves are framed by trailing white leaves, vines and berries and are separated by vertical designs of triangular acanthus leaves flanked by dark wings filled with white berries. A band of square arches and darts contains the rim design at the bottom of the cavetto.

In the central scene there is a large chalet-type mansion at right. A river divides the scene and there is a small sailboat near the building. At left there are tall trees, a stone wall and trailing vines. In the foreground there are three figures; two are seated and one stands nearby. The plate is printed in lavender. The pattern was also made in mulberry.

Marked S.

216

MILESIAN
Made by John Wedge Wood

The edge of the plate shown is detailed with a band of linked darts set over a scalloped line. The rim is covered with a diamond diaper pattern inset with six small scenic vignettes. All show the same towered buildings and lacey trees at right, a stream in the center and a tall graceful elm at left.

A river divides the scene in the center of the dish. In the foreground a girl holding a stick stands on a grassy bank. A man is seated near her at left. He leans against some rocks. Other rocks and tropical foliage including a tall tree that resembles a coconut palm are at right. Across the stream there are domed temple buildings and towers. In the distance the same type of buildings appear in the background.

Marked J. Wedgwood, like GMK. 4276A, c. 1841-60.

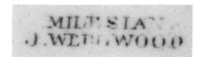

217

MONTES PYRENENSES

Made by John Hulme and Sons

This dish is unevenly scalloped and the white edge is detailed by a band of narrow cartridge forms interspersed with rosettes at eight points. The concave panelled rim is covered with a floral wreath of large open roses, dahlias and other blossoms. The border design covers the cavetto and enters the well.

The center scene is dominated by the towered building at right. It is situated on a platform and overlooks a river. Two men stand on the platform at center. Across the river one sees a large cascade of water descending from the mountain top. These torrents called **gaves** are characteristic of the French side of the Pyrenees which divides France from Spain. At left are houses set on high rocks and pine trees, and the tall sharp peaks of the Pyrenees are in the background.

Marked Hulme and Sons, GMK. 2128, c. 1828-30.

MONTREAL

Made by Davenport

This view of the harbor and the city of Montreal is depicted from Ste. Helene's Island. The steam ship, British North American, paddle wheel at side, Union Jack flying from the prow and stern and its own pennant at midship dominates the river scene. In the foreground there are a canoe with two Indians paddling and a small row boat filled with three sailors in high hats. There are several small sailboats at left on the river and a smaller steamship at right. In the distance one sees the tower of the great Notre Dame church at Place D'Armes in Montreal, other city buildings and smaller church steeples.

The border design consists of a white edge contained by a band of circles and quatrefoils set above a zig-zag triangular line. From this band small beads form a fringe across a stippled area above the floral and scroll design on the lower rim. The dish is printed in sepia.

The source of the view, according to Larson, was a drawing by R.A. Spoule, engraved by W.L. Leney, published in Montreal, 1830, by A. Bourne. The title of the engraving is "View of Montreal from Ste. Helene's Island." The original water color is owned by the McCord Museum at McGill University in Montreal. It shows the spire and square tower of the English cathedral and the French cathedral with square tower and the spire of the old parish church. We illustrate the drawings by Spoule, courtesy of the McCord Museum in Montreal.

Marked with (imp.) anchor, like GMK. 1181, c. 1830.

PLATE III

Montreal
(from St. Helen's Island)
Water colour by R.A. Sproule, 1830.
Collection of McCord Museum,

MONTREAL (cont.)

MOREA

Maker Unknown

The edge of this plate is indented in twelve places and the slight scallops so formed are indicated by a band of beads. A narrow band of stippling and small sprigs is set beneath the beads. The rim design consists of three white architectural motifs that resemble the tops of Corinthian columns. They are flanked by dark swags and are separated by sprays of roses, lilies and sprigs.

The ruins of an ancient Grecian temple are seen in the center of the picture. At left a tall tree rises above fragments of columns, pediments and large flowers which cross the foreground. A tall arch is at right. The usual stream of water divides the scene and a man and his dog are on the near bank and a cow stands on the opposite side of the river. Note that part of the upper edge design on the second dish is omitted and that the plate is not scalloped. This pattern has been noted in brown and medium blue. Morea is in the southern peninsula of Greece.

Marked Stone China.

MOREA (cont.)

NEW YORK
Made by William Adams

Three reserves containing the picture of a youth standing on a river bank with different sailing ships in the background are placed around the stippled rim of this saucer. The reserves alternate with large sun flower halves from which radiate small petals and beaded pendants. The outer edge is detailed with a band of beads.

In the center scene a young couple stand on a flower covered river bank in New Jersey. Across the Hudson one sees the towers and buildings of New York City. Many sailboats, a row boat and an island at right are pictured in the river. This pattern is listed in all books that deal with historical patterns. It is presented in this book for the pictorial interest of the transfer used.

Marked (imp.) Adams, GMK. 18, 1800-64.

PATRAS

(Byron's Illustration)
Made by John Meir

A wreath of palmettos set against a darker stippled ground encircles the upper rim of this scalloped plate. The wreath is contained by a band of darts and beads separated by fine fringe. There are six reserves in the border. They are separated by pairs of vertical bars that are connected at the top by an arch and at the bottom by scallops that contain a parasol design. In the center of each reserve there is an exotic bird; three birds are placed next to ewers and Grecian urns at left, the alternating three are flanked by flowers.

The border design is contained by a shadowy wreath of fringed lines inset with small dark crosses and a band of pale spade shapes and darts.

The central scene contains town buildings at left and includes a domed temple and a tall slim minaret. At right there are tall exotic trees. Two men stand in the center. In the foreground there are rocks. Patras is on the Bay of Patras and is the third largest city in Greece.

Marked IM, GMK. 2632, 1812-36.

PATRAS

Made by Wood and Challinor

The white edges of these twelve sided plates are embossed and small white flowers and scrolls are placed under the raised edges. Three scroll-framed reserves on the large plate and two on the cup plate are placed in a curving net background. Each contains an arch in center, a stone bridge at left, castle buildings in the background, a boat on a river and tall elms on either side. Triangular scroll designs on the bottom of the rim alternate with the vignettes. A bold band of spearpoint under a dark band contains the border pattern on the cavetto.

In the central scene on the large plate the curving stone steps at left lead to the arched entrance of an open square temple which is surmounted by urns. There are two people on the upper landing near the arch. A man is seated on the ground near the large newel at the bottom of the stairs. Two ladies stand at right talking to him. There is a statue of a woman on a pedestal at right and a tall elm behind the statue. Other trees rise at left from either side of the temple. In the distance one sees a lake and a large towered castle.

On the cream pitcher shown there is the same scene but it does not show the couple standing under the arch near the temple. The cup plate has the same scene but omits all human figures.

Marked W. & C., GMK. 4244, c. 1828-43.

PATRAS (cont.)

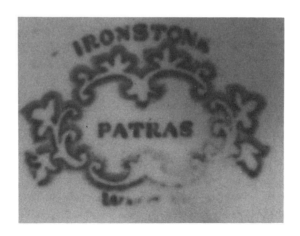

RHODES
Select Sketches
Made by Thomas Dimmock

The edge of this gently scalloped dish was left white and a band of small beads is placed around it. The upper part of the rim design is stippled. Six shield designs filled with a light diamond diaper pattern are connected by foliated scrolls that meet to form a fleur-de-lis. In the curves formed by the scrolls there are small rounded fruits and below the curves the same diamond diaper design fills horizontal reserves that are contained at the base by a narrow band of spearpoint. The shield design covers the cavetto and enters the well. Floral sprays are set between the bases of the shields and create a wreath.

The central scene portrays the harbor of Rhodes, once the leading Greek trade center of the Mediterranean.

Marked D. and Stoneware, GMK. 1297, 1828-59.

228

RHONE

Probably made by John Ridgway

The border design on this blue dish consists of mossy sprigs inset with alternating dark blue and white seven-petalled floral designs that resemble snowflakes. In the central scene are two oar-propelled sailboats in the foreground. There are men and women with wide hats on board as well as nets and other fishing gear.

A tall elm rises behind a pedestal and balustrade at right. In the background there is castle, and in the distance there are towers and clouds which complete the circular picture.

Marked Stone China, like mark 3257, c. 1830-55.

RHONE (cont.)

ROME

(Italian)

Made by William Ridgway

The edge of this unevenly scalloped plate is outlined by a band of white beads on a dark ground. Six shell-like forms each containing a half flower are placed around the beaded band. The concave rim is covered with a diaper pattern of tiny flowers that give a pointe d'esprit effect. Dark two-handled vases flanked by flowers alternate with pairs of large peonies in the center of the rim.

The central scene shows the river Tiber. There are apartment buildings at left. A large boat with canopy is pulled up to the bank in the foreground. At right there is a large round building. In the background at center there is an arched bridge. A large turreted building and other city structures are in the distance.

Marked W.R., GMK. 3301, c. 1830-5.

ROME (cont.)

ROYAL COTTAGE

Made by William Barker & Son

The white edge of this deeply unevenly scalloped platter is defined by a dark band containing white beads. A row of vertical thick fringe is set on a narrow stippled band at the top of the concave rim. The rest of the rim and the cavetto are covered with large pairs of wild roses, tea roses, leaves, buds and sprigs. At top and bottom there are matching sprays of dahlias, peonies, poppies, sprigs and forget-me-nots.

The romantic two story cottage of the title sits on its extensive grounds at left center. In front of the cottage a tall elm tree rises from a flower covered rocky bank at the left of a stream that bisects the scene. An arched bridge crosses the scene and the water falls toward the foreground where a pair of swans are floating. At right there is a very large urn filled with overscaled flowers and a tall willow-like tree. In the background a sailboat crosses the river and in the distance there are towered buildings and many tall mountain peaks. (This same pattern shown on the small dish was issued under the name Tonquin about 1930 with the backstamp of Clarice Cliff, Royal Staffordshire. It is marked like GMK. 4172).

Marked W. Barker and Son, like GMK. 256A, c. 1850-60.

ROYAL COTTAGE (cont.)

"RURAL SCENE"

Made by Davenport

The edge of this plate is white and is scalloped, and a band of beads sets off the white edge. A thin band of stippling is at the very top of the rim. The rest of the border design consists of foliated reserves with double shell-like crowns that are filled with egg-crate diapering. Pairs of flowers are placed between the reserves.

A pair of cows and two sheep are in the foreground of the central picture. Tall elms rise on either side from the bushy banks of a river. A man fishes from the right bank in the center. In the background there are city buildings and a bridge, and in the far distance one sees a tower perched on top of a mountain peak.

Marked Davenport, GMK. 1181A, 1836.

RURAL SCENERY
Made by Bathwell & Goodfellow

The edge of this blue dish is gently lobed and is decorated by a band of small arches. The concave rim is covered with a design of three large open roses with dark white-veined leaves that alternate with three long flowing foliated white scrolls set over pairs of dark sweet williams.

In the central scene a girl sits on a platform. Next to her is a wooden bucket. She is placed in the shade of a large tree. In the background there are farm buildings, a fence and trees. In the distance at left there is a church and a tower.

Marked (imp.) as above, GMK. 294, 1818-23.

RURAL SCENERY
Made by Davenport

The border design of this pattern appears under the open loop-laced edge and white embossed basket-weave edge. Four vignettes containing a scene of a small cottage set in the shade of a tall elm are set around the rim. They are framed with scrolls and flowers. Alternating scenes show long low farm buildings.

In the central scene a girl sits on the grass in the foreground. She wears a little sloping oval hat. She holds a baby or a lamb on her knees. In the background there is a cottage with thatched roof.

Marked as above and (imp.) an anchor. Like GMK. 1181A, c. 1805-60.

RUSTIC SCENERY
Made by Joseph Clementson

The stippled panelled rim of this twelve sided light blue and white plate is covered with leaves. Six oval reserves each containing the picture of a rustic cottage, three with a fence at right and three with a fence at left are set around the border.

A vine covered with sprigs and leaves encircles the central scene of a girl standing with a boy sitting on the ground at her left and a water jug placed on the ground at her right. In the distance are a cottage and trees that resemble those seen in the border reserve.

The scene on the side of the master salt dish shown presents a man seated on a rock. He holds a long pole with a fish net attached at the top. There is a creel on the ground behind him at left. A small girl stands next to him at right.

Marked J. Clementson, GMK. 910A, 1839-64.

RUSTIC SCENERY (cont.)

"SCROLL FROND BORDER"

Made by Charles Meigh

This dish is fourteen sided and the panelled concave rim is covered with a dotted background. White foliated scrolls shadowed by a darker stippled line form a wreath around the rim. A band of beads is set at the top edge and a circle of triangles and interlaced beaded lines form a short fringe on the cavetto.

A ruined church is in the middle of the scene. It is set on the far bank of a stream that divides the picture. In the foreground there are small rapids and rocks and a pair of elms rise from the right bank. At left a man in a white coat holds a fishing pole. He is standing on a grassy bank. A boy and a dog are seated near him under the shade of a tall elm.

Marked French China, like GMK. 27183, 1835-49.

SEASONS
Made by Thomas Godwin

The edge of this blue and white soup plate is defined by a band of white-edged beads. The border pattern consists of large snail-like scrolls that surround the rim. They are placed over a background of a vine which carries sprigs and leaves that resemble wheat.

There are four shepherds in the central scene. Two are at left, one sits on a hummock and the other, holding a baby lamb, stands near him. The other pair are seated at right.

There are sheep in the middle ground. At left there is a sort of tent which also appears in the backstamp. Rolling hills, many shade trees, and mountain peaks in the distance complete the picture.

Marked T. Godwin, mark not listed but resembles in part GMK. 1730B, 1834-54.

SEINE

Made by John Tams

The rim of this dish is covered with a horizontal basket weave design. It is contained at the base by a row of scallops and short diagonal lines interrupted by six pairs of shield designs that resemble fleur-de-lis. Garlands of small flowers cover the lower rim and descend into the cavetto.

A man punts a flat boat on a river in the center scene. In the foreground on the near bank a woman in a bonnet, shawl and long dress stands with a man wearing a frock coat and high hat. At right there are tall towered buildings. At left the usual tall elm rises from the ground beside a curved pine tree. In the distance down river there are city buildings and an arched bridge.

Marked J. Tams, GMK. 3792, c. 1875.

SEVRES

Made by I. Harris

The gently scalloped edge of this cup plate is decorated with a wreath of five-petalled stylized flowers framed with five pointed trellis patterns of leaves and connected by two C-scrolls. A band of tiny buds forms arches around the flowers. The lower part of the rim is covered with the same floral and leaf patterns in large scale, reversed from top to bottom, and set under the arches formed by the buds.

Two large elms are seen on a hillside in the central scene. Parts of a bridge, a building and mountains can be seen at the extreme right in the background. In the foreground there are several small white flowers or stones and some ferns.

Marked (imp.) as above and "Sevres".

SHIELD

Made by James Edward

This twelve sided dark blue plate has a panelled concave rim printed with a light blue design of cartouche shapes, the shields of the title (used also on the backstamp). These shields are placed over a pedestal of foliated scrolls and flanked by eagles. The shield designs are separated by a double circular design composed of foliated scrolls.

A wreath of passion flowers and scrolls frames the central scene which is dominated by a dark arched bridge set over a deep ravine. In the foreground a man leans over a low parapet to look down into the gorge. The ruins of a Roman temple are situated on a high cliff in the left background and in the right background there is a church-like building with a tower. A tall leafy flowering tree rises from the right stanchion of the bridge. The moon or sun is at upper left.

Marked as above, printed with Saxon China, and (imp.) "Real Ironstone", mark not located but resembles GMK. 1447, 1842-51.

SPANISH BEAUTIES

Probably made by Deakin and Sons

The uppermost part of the rim of this gently scalloped plate is covered with sprigs and trios of small flowers. A design consists of floral shapes flanked by trellis-filled wings set above two large scrolls and a pair of flowers. The scrolls are placed over a five arm spoke that resemble fire-crackers and they separate the scenic cartouches. All the reserves contain the same scene of balustrades at right, a river with two sailboats in the center, a tree and bushes at left and a large turreted castle in the back-ground. A garland of flowers frames the central scene.

In the central picture a man in Elizabethan costume is seated at left. He plays a guitar to serenade a lady holding a book, who sits on a bench in the ciddle of the scene. Another woman stands behind him. A very large urn filled with flowers is set upon a table at right behind a balustrade. A tall square arch topped with urns is in the background and so are tall elms. Also in the background there is a river on which boats are sailing. There are castles and mountains in the distance. The plate is printed in medium blue.

This same pattern was recorded in a black and white printing and it was backstamped Sevilla. See Book I page 414.

Like GMK. 1218, 1833-41.

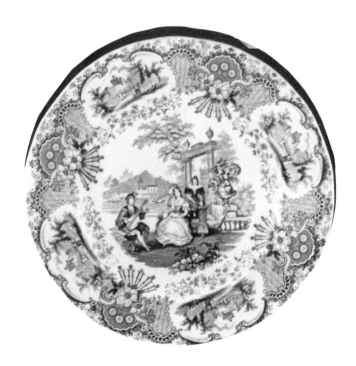

SPANISH BEAUTIES (cont.)

SUSPENSION BRIDGE

Made by Enoch Wood and Sons

This plate bears the same title and the maker's backstamp as that shown in Book I page 424, but the border is different. The outer edge is detailed with a row of dark and light straight lines. The stippled rim is patterned with six lace-edged curved reserves filled with tiny triple dots that give a pointe d'esprit effect. Large flowers are placed next to the reserves, and sprigs enter the dotted ground. The six floral patterns are separated by flame-like foliated fleur-de-lis. A wide band of tiny narrow lines and dots covers the cavetto. The central scene, framed by a wreath of running wide U-scrolls and beads, is also different from that shown in the first book.

The cup plate bears a different bridge scene and part of the rim pattern has been omitted so that only the tips of the lacey border of the reserves and part of the flowers were used. The rim and center designs are separated by the wreath used around the central part of the larger plate.

Marked E.W. & S., GMK. 4260, c. 1818-46.

"SWISS FARM"

Probably made by Enoch Wood & Sons

The cup plate photographed has an edge detailed with small diamond pendants. The scene shows a farm house with a long angled stairway to the entrance. There are outbuildings and large barrels and tent-like structures at left. (These may be nets drying). There is a small figure of a woman in the foreground.

Marked (imp.) Wood and the number 8. Mark not located, c. 1840.

"SWISS LAKE AND VILLAGE"

Made by Davenport

The dishes shown are all the same pattern but Davenport used two different borders. The title given above is used to catalog. It does not appear in a backstamp. Perhaps Davenport issued these plates as two different patterns.

The border on the pink sauce stand and on the black and white plate, both with white embossed edges, consists of a very dark upper rim set against the white edge. Small white rosettes are placed in the dark field. A wreath of foliated scrolls alternating with baroque lattice-filled scrolls surrounds the upper rim. Large floral designs separated by sprigs are placed in the arches formed by the scrolls. The scene on the stand presents a sailboat pulled up to the shore of a lake. There are large dark rocks in the foreground and a tall elm at left. In the distance there are village buildings huddled under very tall mountains. There are castle ruins and a tower on top of one of the mountain peaks. The scene on the plate shows a lake at center, a road with a guardrail at left and a village placed at the base of the mountains in the distance.

The ten inch dish, printed in soft blue carries the exact scene as described above, but the stippled border is covered with fine vertical undulating lines which continue over the cavetto and end in a saw-tooth circle around the well. The white edge is embossed and a printed twisted white rope is placed under the embossing.

The next dish shown is also blue and white and has the same border just described but the central scene is framed by tall elms and bushes in both the left and right foreground. Two men are in a flat boat in the center; one stands and is poling the craft and the other bends over the side to pull upon a floating round cork-edged net. In the middle ground there are many buildings of a large town. There is a tiled roof pavilion on the waterfront, and many towers and a bridge in the left distance. The tall Alpine peaks fill the distant background.

The cup plate in this pattern was presented in Book I, on page 389 under the title Rhine River Scene. It is printed in pink and has no border. The scene is in reverse from the two large plates with the guardrail at right. (Illustrated overscaled).

Marked (imp.) Davenport, dated with an anchor 1836, GMK. 1181A.

SWISS LAKE AND VILLAGE (cont.)

SWISS LAKE AND VILLAGE (cont.)

TEMPLE

Made by Thomas Edwards

The twelve sided panelled concave rim of this dish is covered with a meandering pattern of wave-like lines. A wreath of angular beaded scrolls, all directed to the right, separate pairs of wild roses. A wreath of sprigs is placed around the cavetto.

The ruins of the temple of the title are at right set high on a river bank. At left there are two small figures in peasant costume. They are placed on a steep bank. A tall elm rises at the center. In the distance there are other buildings, a temple and some stony peaks.

Marked T. Edwards, (imp.) Porcelain Opaque, mark not located.

"THAMES RIVER SCENE"

Possibly made by Enoch Wood and Sons

The border pattern appears on the collar and lid of this orchid and white teapot. It consists of five-petalled flowers with very dark leaves which alternate with grapes set in a stippled ground.

The river scene on the sides of the body presents the skyline of a large city in the background. One sees spires, a fortress with tower and a large domed building at left. A small boat, with three passengers, is poled by a standing man in the center of the foreground. At left two women stand on a park-like bank near a seated man who is fishing. At right in the foreground there is part of a rustic fence and a tall elm, and at left there is a large white flowering bush.

Marked (imp.) WOOD, like mark 4247 but probably made later by Enoch Wood and Sons, 1818-46.

"TYROLEAN SCENE"

Made by William Ridgway

This border of scalloped lace from which tiny sprigs extend towards the well was used by Ridgway on a series done for the American market.

The central scene on this dish is European. There is an ornate cottage at right surrounded by tall pine trees. A river divides the scene and at left across the river one sees a church with ornamental spires. A girl in Austrian costume stands holding a small jug and a little dog stands in front of her in the center of the scene. In the foreground a large swan swims in a pond.

Marked W. Ridgway and Improved Granite China, GMK. 3300, 1830-4.

UDINA

Made by Joseph Clementson

Peonies are placed in baroque scrolled reserves on the rims of this octagonal platter and dinner plate. Bell flowers are placed on a very dark ground between the reserves at the top edge, and white rosettes are used to separate the reserves at the bottom. A wreath of scrolls and roses contains the border design in the cavetto.

Snowy Alpine peaks form the background of the central scene which contains a castle with tall slender towers at left. At the right there is a steep bank from which tall elms grow. At the foot of the bank there are four persons. A river divides the scene and a bridge crosses the water in the distance.

The plate is printed in a warm gray, the platter in sepia.

Marked J. Clementson, also marked with a Phoenix Bird and Ironstone, GMK. 910A, 1839-64. (The second mark shown is that of an importer in the United States).

UDINA (cont.)

UNION

Made by William Ridgway, Son & Co.

A border design of a trailing vine with stylized leaves and berries covers the rim of this dish (10″), and it is contained in the well by a wreath of diamonds and short spearpoint. The same wreath forms the band that encircles the outer edge of the blue and white plate.

The center scene is dominated by a large urn with wide basin at top which is filled with fruits and fern fronds. The statues of a girl and boy are at its base which is set upon a tiered pedestal. At right classic temples are placed upon the sides of a hill overlooking the river that divides the scene. At left there are steps, part of a fence and a pair of tall elms; in the left distance one sees the buildings and towers of a town. In the far distance there are mountain peaks. Clouds above complete the circular picture.

Marked W.R.S & Co. GMK. 3308, 1838-48.

Also marked (imp.), a royal coat of arms with the shield inscribed Opaque Granite China, W.R. & Co., GMK. 3303, 1834+.

UNION (cont.)

VALENCIENNES

Made by Enoch and Edward Wood

The border design on this plate consists of an outer narrow band of a diamond diaper inset with quatrefoil. The same band but trimmed with scallops contains the design at the well. Between the bands a vine bearing three maple-type serrated leaves and fronds of ovals that resemble the design of peacock feathers encircles the rim. A wreath of spearpoint is placed around the cavetto.

The central scene shows two men standing on a small rustic bridge. They hold fishing nets on poles. The bridge connects the bank with an elm at left and a stone building with a water wheel at right. A river divides the scene in the center of the picture. In the right background there are trees and a tall Gothic tower. In the left distance one sees other towers and mountain peaks. Valenciennes is in France (in French Flanders) and is a textile center.

Marked E. and E. Wood, and printed Imperial China and (imp.) Pearl China, 1818-46.

VAN DYKE

Made by Samuel Alcock

The scalloped rim of this dish is slightly indented. The outer edge is decorated with a band of small dark rosettes. The distinctive zig-zag rim pattern is composed from triangular stippled areas filled with sprigs that are placed around the upper rim and also on the lower rim leaving a white zig-zag area in the middle. Small feathery sprigs descend into the well and form a band of arches and rosettes that invades the well.

Towering Gothic ruins are at right in the center scene. What appears to be a part of a large column is in the right middle ground. An arched bridge or aqueduct can be seen in the distance. There is water in the foreground and tall large lilies and overscaled ruffled peonies are at left and descend into the foreground.

The cup plate has part of the border design but the feathery sprigs framing the central scene are distinguishing elements. The scene differs in the building shown at right but the floral design at left is the same.

Marked S.A. & Co., GMK. 75, c. 1830-59. (This pattern was listed as Unknown Scenic 21 page 712 in Vol. 1).

VASE

Maker Unknown

The edge of this scalloped platter is decorated with a band of diamonds and sprigs. The pattern on the rim presents geometric angular flower shapes with realistic leaves that alternate with an oval design containing a dark center inset with a rosette topped with a triangular crown and flanked by large leaves and sprigs.

The vase of the title is set upon a flat stone pediment in the right foreground. Realistic flowers and leaves are placed on the ground nearby. A sailboat can be seen at center on a river that divides the scene. Across the water there are towered buildings. A tall lacey elm rises from the balustraded terrace behind the vase.

Marked Stoneware.

VENETIAN GARDENS

Maker Unknown

The edge of this pink and white scalloped dish is outlined with white beads. The border pattern is dominated by three large pairs of peonies which alternate with three fleuron studded shields. These designs are set in a field of narrow vertical lines which cross the cavetto, and are separated by baroque pendants and small flowers.

A wreath of beads surrounds the central scene. The garden of the title is depicted by a flower laden arch composed of scrolls topped with a fan shaped shade upon a rounded base which resembles a lantern. There are covered urns and some stone steps in the foreground. In the background, seen through the arch, there is an imposing columned building with a wide pediment surmounted by a statue.

VENICE
Made by Enoch Wood and Sons

A pattern from this series is shown in Book I, page 351 (Oberwessel on Rhine). Here is that plate and its backstamp. The border design of sprays of white ferns alternates with a sepia transfer of dainty ferns and sprigs. The scalloped edges are defined by a band of tiny crosses alternating with rosettes. The borders in the pattern are stippled in a creamy yellow and the central scenes are sepia.

The cup plate shows a tower at right and a sailboat in the left foreground. Ledecker named this pattern "Venice". The cup plate is not backstamped.

Marked E. Wood & Sons, GMK. 4261, 1818-46.

VERONA

Made by Edward Challinor

A band of small dark beads surrounds the edge of this saucer. The border background is stippled. Four sprig designs composed of many white trefoils separate facing pairs of scalloped cartouches. Two reserves contain a large stylized blossom and leaves, and the other pair show a scene of a fallen tree, a river, an elm and a tower in the left distance. The border pattern is contained at the bottom by scallops and tiny beads.

A wide river divides the scene in the center. In the foreground at the base of a tall elm there are pieces of fallen columns. In the middle distance at right there are towered buildings. Three small figures including a woman wearing a head shawl are near the structures. At left in the distance across the stream there are some other buildings and tall mountains.

Marked E.C., GMK. 835, 1842-67.

VERONA

Made by Minton

The upper half of the scalloped rim of this plate is covered with a net and small bead design on a dark stippled ground. The border pattern consists of horizontal scrolled arches placed over garlands of small flowers which alternate with large single blossoms placed over scrolled bases.

In the center scene there are large romantic ruins at left and in the center a man and woman stand on a rounded bank in the middle ground. Another person lies on the ground at their feet. A cherub fountain sends water into the air nearby. In the background there are other ruins and arches, a body of water and islands, and in the distance there are peaked mountains. In the foreground one sees parts of a fallen stone column festooned with overscaled flowers. This transfer design is printed in a dark greyish green.

Marked M., it is like GMK. 2690, c. 1822-36. Also (imp.) in a cartouche "Improved Stone China."

VILLA SCENERY

Possibly made by Deakin & Bailey

Twelve embossed flowers mark the twelve scallops on the edge of the concave rim of this dish. The upper part of the rim has three scrolled reserves filled with honeycomb diapering. Passion flowers set in a bouquet of daisies and roses alternate with large peonies around the rim. Sprigs form the floral designs and enter the cavetto.

In the center foreground of the picture a large bird sits on a stone platform at left; he is pecking at some over-scaled flowers at right. There is an equally overscaled blossom at left. In the middle ground at right there is a gazebo surmounted by a statue. A river divides the background and there is a building with a tall tower at left. A large bird is depicted in the backstamp and probably is the element in identifying the pattern.

Marked D. & B., see Godden page 715, GMK. 4420, c. 1828-30.

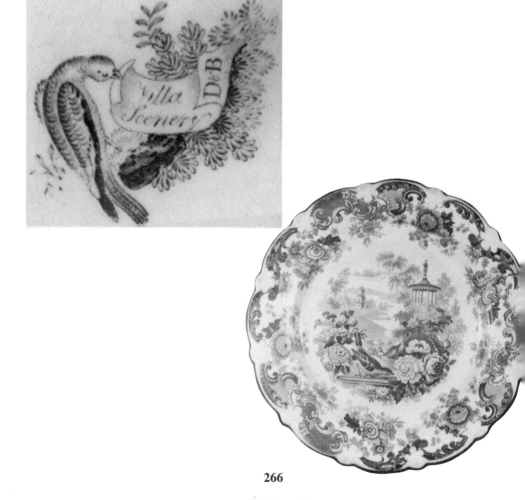

VIRGINIA

Possibly made by Enoch Wood

The border design on this saucer consists of triple beaded scroll-framed reserves each containing a pair of large dahlias. They are separated by a diamond trellis covered with beaded scrolls flanking a central flower. At the bottom of the border a zig-zag is made to contain the border pattern of small flowers and pendants which form a spearpoint design around the well. In the central scene a girl and boy in Edwardian costume stand at left and face a plant stand filled with large potted plants. There is a gazebo in the background.

Marked (imp.) W., could be Wood, GMK. 4250, c. 1830 plus.

WALMER

Possibly made by Elijah Hodgkinson

The rim of this ten sided sepia plate is panelled and the background is stippled. Vignettes depicting a man in high hat and a lady dressed in white, carrying a shawl and wearing a large plumed hat are at center in front of a rustic white bench. There is a leaping white greyhound at right, an urn at left and a huge tent in the background. The reserves are separated by large white ivy leaves which also garland the upper edge which is framed by a double row of stringing and garland around the cavetto under a duplicate double band.

In the center scene the man and lady stand. Two small children are seated on the ground near them. The picture is dominated by the large statue of a man astride a rearing horse. There are tall elms behind the statue. In the left background there is a castle with four elaborate Gothic towers, and in the distance there is a lake or view and many mountain peaks.

This pattern was also made in Flow Blue.

Walmer was a former district near Kent, England. Walmer castle, built by Henry VIII is there. It was and is a popular seaside resort visited by many famous people. The Duke of Wellington died there. In 1935 it was incorporated into the city of Deal.

Marked E.H. and (imp.) Stone. Could be one of three potters. See Godden page 716, 1851 plus.

WARWICK

Made by Podmore Walker & Co.

This dish is twelve sided and the rim is slightly concave. The upper part of the rim is covered with a dark ground filled with scrolls and flowers which descend into the lower rim which has a lighter background. Oval shield designs containing large covered urns with double dark wing-shaped handles are placed around the border.

A Swiss chalet with bold crockets is in the center. Behind it one sees tall Gothic towers. At right there are slender elms and in the right distance an arched bridge crosses a stream.

Marked as above, (imp.), c. 1834-59.

WARWICK

Made by John Ridgway & Co.

The edge of this dish is lobed and the concave rim with a background of narrow concentric lines is covered with a Gothic design of six large teardrops or keyholes flanked by large foliated scrolls that meet and form a spade at top. The bottoms of the teardrops are decorated with scrolls and leaves that enter the cavetto.

In the central picture a large castle with high walls and towers, with very small window openings near the top, is set high above the left bank of a stream. A bridge crosses the water in the middle of the scene and tall elms rise at right. A boat filled with three figures is in the left foreground. Dark clouds complete the circular picture.

Marked J. Ridgway & Co., GMK. 3259A, Reg. date Oct. 1847.

WASHINGTON

Made by Clementson & Young

The concave rim of this ten sided dish is covered with a design that resembles the weaving patterns found on coverlets. Ten vertical bars inset with small horizontal bars are placed between cartouches that contain a large eagle perched on a rock, a star above his head and a ship at sea behind him.

In the center six small figures are placed on the bank of a river. A gazebo is at left and a tall elm rises at extreme left. In the right distance there are towered buildings that resemble a fortress. The Stars and Stripes flies from the tallest tower.

Marked as above, GMK. 911, 1845-7.

WINDSOR

Made by Mellor, Venables & Co.

The plate photographed is fourteen sided and the panelled rim is covered with narrow concentric lines overlaid with a pattern of twining stems covered with morning glories, tendrils and leaves. The border enters the cavetto and is contained in the well by a band of double flattened ovals separated by vertical dark bars ending in tiny triangles.

In the center scene Windsor castle with its famous tower, a flag flying from its top, is in the background and overlooks the Thames. A boat with enclosed rear section, propelled by oarsmen, and sporting pennants fore and aft is in the middle ground. In the foreground a trio of costumed figures is on the bank at right. Tall trees and cascading vines are at extreme right. Clouds complete the circular picture.

Marked as above, and (imp.) Ironstone, GMK. 2646, dated August 1849.

WREATH AND FLOWERS
Made by Enoch Wood & Sons

This soup plate is unevenly scalloped and sprays of ferns centered with flowers and dark leaves cover the concave rim. The wreath of the title, which includes a dark vase at upper right and a dark covered urn on a pedestal supported by scrolled treillage at left, surrounds the scene of a Gothic church ruin, tall trees that resemble palms, a river and mountain peaks.

Marked E.W. & S., GMK. 4260, c. 1818-46.

WREATH AND FLOWERS (cont.)

Genre Category

ACCEPTED

Made by the Sunderland Pottery

The border pattern on this saucer consists of three stippled wide, scalloped reserves, flanked by large blossoms. A beaded ribbon is placed under the dark sections and continues to the upper rim forming white arches topped with trophies (a target, quiver arrow and a hunting horn). The white areas are contained at the cavetto by snail-like curves.

A girl and boy holding hands are seated on a bench in the central scene. There is a spinning wheel behind her and she holds a parasol in her right hand. He wears Scottish jerkin, kilt and tam. In the distance there is a church, and trees form a circular frame around the scene.

Marked (imp.) Dixon Phillips & Co. GMK. 3747, c. 1840-65.

"ARCHERY"

Made by Elkin, Knight & Bridgwood

The gently scalloped concave rim of this cup plate is covered with vertical quills. The edge is defined by a band of small ovals and darts. The border pattern consists of two large sprays, each containing an oval target set behind a large open rose. The sprays are separated by lightly stippled morning glories, buds, and flowerlets.

Two young boys holding bows stand in the foreground of the central scene. In the middle distance there is a fence and behind that, there is a church at right and a large house at left. Elm trees rise at the left. There are bushes that extend to the foreground and overscaled morning glories are seen at right..

Mark E.K.B. GMK. 1464, c. 1827-40.

ARCHERY
Made by Job and John Jackson

The edge of the saucer photographed is outlined with a band of beads. The border design consists of a trio of baroque scrolls which contain a trellis design and are decorated with a few flowers at the lower left. These alternate with a large peony-type blossom. The upper part of the rim is covered with a diaper pattern consisting of tiny flower forms which give a point d' esprit affect.

In the central scene stand two ladies dressed in long gowns and large hats. They hold long bows and arrows. Behind the women there is a circular tent topped with a pennant. At right there is a lake and a small boat is sailing on it and a church-like building is in the background. Tall elms are on either side of the scene; bushes, leaves, overscaled flowers in the foreground complete the design.

The cream pitcher has the wreath of beads at the top of the collar and part of the point d' esprit in the same area. One side of the cream pitcher bears the picture of the two women with their bows and arrows. The other side shows only a floral bouquet.

Marked Jackson's. Like GMK. 2156, c. 1831-5.

ARCHERY (cont.)

BAVARIAN

Made by Samuel Ginder & Co.

The white edge of this dish is outlined with a diamond dotted band and small dark beads. The reserves on the border contain a pair of rabbits, one white and one shaded, and are framed by large flowers and leaves. The space between the rabbit reserves are filled with small geometric patterned flowers and leaves.

In the center scene, which is wreathed by a narrow band of arches and beads, a small girl dressed in shepherdess hat, blouse and skirt, holds a flag set on a long pole. She stands under an arch of flowers. There is part of a barn or shed at left and there are mountains in the distance.

Marked Ginder. Like GMK. 1702, c. 1811-43.

CHEVY CHASE
Made by Enoch Wood & Sons

The scalloped edge of this plate is accented by a narrow scalloped band of sprigs and beads. The border design consists of four stippled reserves picturing huntsmen on horse back. One pair shows two men, one with a horn over his arm and the other waving his cap, with hounds that have treed their quarry at the left. The other pair depicts two men astride, one with a feathered hat waves a whip, the other wears a hunting cap. The hounds are racing at right. The scenes are separated by white reserves that contain a hunting bag, a rifle and a dead bird, all hanging from a rosette. The patterns are framed by a scrolled band of the same sprigs and beads that decorate the edge.

In the central scene the man with the plumed hat is astride a black steed and holds a falcon on his wrist. A woman who rides sidesaddle is seated beside him on a caparisoned white horse. On the ground a groom kneels and holds the hounds. A dead bird lies on the grass. There is a very large vase on a pedestal at the right center and a balustrade extends from behind the vase to the extreme right.

Marked E.W. & S. GMK. 4260, c. 1818-46.

FORGET-ME-NOT

Made by William Ridgway and Co.

On this old bowl a girl is portrayed sitting under a leafy tree. She wears a flowing white gown with a high dark sash and holds a spaniel close to her side. The background consists of meadows, trees and a cottage. There are mountains in the distance.

The border pattern appears on the upper inside rim of the bowl and consists of four large open flowers flanked by scrolls and separated by sprigs and forget-me-nots.

Mark W.R. and Co. GMK. 3303A, c. 1835-54.

HANNIBAL PASSING THE ALPS
Made by Knight, Elkin & Co.

The large blue platter photographed is scalloped and the uppermost part of the rim is covered with a trellis design. Pendant sprays of flowers are placed around the rim and form arched reserves, two of which carry scenes of an elephant, trunk upraised, carrying a group of men with spears and led by a man on a horse and a standing warrior with a spear. There are stylized pine trees at left and the Alps in the distance. The other pair of scenes in the border present a warrior on horseback who carries a pennant or standard. At left in the background there is an elephant, another horse and a standing man. The Alps are in the distance and the pine tree is at right. The scenic reserves alternate with a pair of large dahlias, leaves and sprays.

In the center scene a Carthaginian soldier on horseback is about to run a spear through a Roman warrior who has been thrown to the ground and whose horse rears in fright. An elephant carrying a covered howdah is behind the horseman. Soldiers appear in the mountain pass in the left background and others are at right coming up a hill. There are pine trees on either side of the scene which is really dominated by the towering snow covered Alps.

The red saucer, which is shown in Book I on page 725 as unknown Genre 11 (UG11) is not scalloped. It is marked with the impressed eagle, the shield and No. 26 (shown). The border design is the same as that on the platter but two vignettes are different and shown a man carrying a long spear as he rides a galloping dark horse. The central scene on the dish is that which appears in the border of the platter of the mounted man carrying a pennant.

The cup plate which is printed in sepia and is scalloped has the border design with a slight variation of the horseman. The center scene shows a Carthaginian archer perched on a rocky hill. There are pine trees at left, flowers in the foreground and mountains in the background.

The scalloped plate (10") is printed in sepia. The central picture shows a Roman soldier attacking an elephant while an archer at left aims at the Roman. In the background there is a very tall double arched bridge and Hannibal's soldiers and elephants have marched across it and are on a path at upper right.

Marked (imp.) with an eagle. c. 1826-46. (See Coysh Dictionary pg. 170).

HANNIBAL (cont.)

HANNIBAL (cont.)

HAWKING
Made by J. & M.P. Bell & Co.

The edge of this soup plate is defined by a band of white beads that contain dark center dots. Three scenic cartouches are set around the rim and contain a picture of an arch and balustrade at left, a river and a pair of swans. White floral wreaths are at the top and the bottom of the border and are separated by a stippled band decorated with a narrow twining vine.

In the center scene a noble lady is seated side saddle on a caprisoned white horse, and she holds a falcon on her upraised right hand which is protected by a gauntlet. A page, at left leads the horse and a man stands at the right. Both are clothed in Elizabethan jackets, breeches, and tall boots, and the man wears a large plumed hat.

Behind the group there is a very large castle set on top of a rocky hill. There are trees at either side of the picture and in the distance one sees a church spire and a mountain.

Marked J. & M.P.B. & Co. GMK. 318, c. 1850-70.

HOP (THE)

Made by Elijah Jones

The edges of the saucer and cream pitcher shown are scalloped and are defined by a white line covered with tiny beads. A band of intersecting semi-circles covers the upper part of the border. Small triangular flowers are set in the intersections created above. The border design consists of groups of large hops that separate scenic vignettes of a boy who carries a pole covered with hops. He is kneeling in front of a tall, wide-rimmed basket. A woman stands on the other side of the basket and is pulling hops from the vine and putting them into the receptacle. Both designs enter the well.

The central scenes differ but all contain a character who carries a pole of hops or carries the basket of hops on his back or works at stripping the hops from the pole into the larger basket. Hops are harvested in the fall.

Marked E.J. GMK. 2214, c. 1828-48.

THE HOP (cont.)

HUNSTMAN
Made by William Adams & Son

The top part of the rim of this scalloped saucer is decorated with alternating dark and light vertical bands that resemble cartridge forms. Three scrolled reserves are set around the concave rim and contain a picture of a fleeing fox running through the countryside. The reserves are joined by scalloped floral bands and there are four white fleur-de-lys shapes set over the band in three sections around the rim. A wreath of snail-like scrolls under the bands, and stylized flowers under the foxes surround the central scene which is composed of two mounted men dressed in hunting hats and jackets, pants and boots. Two dogs are in the foreground. In the background there are pine trees and in the distance at right one sees a church steeple and mountains.

Marked (imp.) Adams. GMK. 18, c. 1800-64.

MANDOLINE
Made by Samuel Ginder & Co.

The edge of this plate is unevenly scalloped and is decorated with a white band of oval beads. The upper part of the concave rim is stippled and is patterned with a diaper design of small oval cartridge forms. The rest of the border pattern consists of six baroque-scrolled, floral shields separated by treillage surmounted with pairs of large flowers. The border pattern covers the cavetto and is contained in the well by a wreath of fringe and double tassels.

In the central scene a man and woman are seated on a bench beneath a large flowering tree. He plays a trumpet and she holds open the music sheets for him. At left there is a Gothic garden house or folly. A river divides the scene in the background and in the distance there are tall buildings and mountain peaks.

Marked S. Ginder & Co. Exact GMK. 1702, c. 1811-43.

MEXICAN

Maker Unknown

This plate is gently and unevenly scalloped. The upper part of the border is stippled. A wreath of large flowers, fern-like leaves, sprays and buds covers the lower rim and crosses the cavetto.

In the center an Indian woman in a shawl carrying a baby on her back talks to a man who wears a large basket-like hat and a cape over a tunic. A child stands between the couple. All three figures are barefoot. In the left center ground a man rides a panierred mule, and at right, in the middle distance, a man is bent over and carries a large flat basket on his back. There are exotic trees at left and palm leaves in the foreground. A smoking volcanic peak is in the distance at right.

Marked *J.L.*

MILITARY SKETCHES
Made by Joseph Heath & Co.

The background of the border design on this plate is covered with a diamond diaper net that extends into the well and is contained there by a scalloped wreath that frames the central scene. Four large sprays of flowers are placed around the rim and alternate with four small scenes of military tents.

In this dish the central scene portrays three mounted Hussars who are approaching a tree at the base of which is a large stone bust of a general or a king. In the background across a river there are buildings, towers, and high mountain peaks. A tall leafy elm rises at right and arches across the scene. Clouds complete the circular picture.

Marked J.H. & Company. GMK. 1994A, c. 1828-41.

NAPOLEON'S VICTORIES
Made by Skinner & Walker

Note the difference in the border design between this pattern and Mason's Napoleon. Pictured on the stippled border of this wash basin are two scenes each of Napoleon seated on a rearing horse alternating with Napoleon seated, arms folded, on a folding metal camp chair. The white flower strewn reserves between the vignettes are crowned by war trophies. The ribbon form that encloses these patterns carries the names of ten battle sites of Napoleon's career, ranging from Arcola to Wagram.

The central scene appears to be in Egypt. At left there are palm trees, a scimitar crowned tower and the crenelated walls of a fortress. Napoleon on horseback leads his troops in the left foreground. Also in the foreground a fallen French soldier lies across part of a broken cannon.

Marked (imp.) S&W's Queen's Wear, Stockton. GMK. 3569, 1870-80.

Note: Coysh states that this pattern was also made by William Smith & Co. 1822-55, subsequently by G. Skinner & Co., then Skinner and Walker.

PHILOSOPHER

Maker Unknown

Three cartouches are set into the border of this dish; each contains a globe, two large books, quill pens, a scroll, and an overscaled flower at left. The cartouches are set against a stippled background covered with white flowerettes. A bird perched on a spray of dark leaves is set between the scenic reserves; small scrolls encircle the cavetto. The dish is printed in black.

The philosopher of the title, dressed in cap and long robe, sits on a folding chair, his right hand resting on a large table. A small boy stands at the teacher's knee and points to a telescope on the table. Books are behind the telescope; there is a standing globe at left. The scene takes place in a flowering arbor. In the distance one sees a winding river, some towers and mountains.

ROYAL GROUP

Maker Unknown

There is no border design on this small cream pitcher, but there is a row of diamonds on the handle and this may be part of a rim pattern. The Royal Group of the title are afloat in a small boat in the foreground. Two ladies, one holding a parasol, are seated in the craft and a man stands in the stern and poles it forward. A white swan swims near the boat in the foreground. At left, there is a tall narrow building with five pointed towers on top. There are stylized flowers at left and a realistic tree and plants at right. Inside the spout (not shown) part of the base design from the building is shown. This same center scene was noted at an antique show on a pitcher titled "Cygnet".

RUTH BOAZ
Made by Petrus Regout

This bowl is printed in purple and the scene on the side and in the center depict the Biblical account of Ruth, a childless widow who followed her mother-in-law, Naomi, to Bethlehem. Ruth worked in the field owned by a wealthy man named Boaz. He married her and she gave birth to Obed, grandfather of David.

The border pattern appears inside the top of the bowl and consists of arched reserves filled with a stippled field and containing sprays of flowers. Foliated scrolls at the bottom form a wreath around the central scene.

Marked P. Regout and Co., Maastricht.

SOUVENIR
Made by John Ridgway

A bank of white beads surrounds the edge of this dish. The border is covered with a dotted diamond-diaper design. Scrolled sections, filled with vermicelli, placed over a large open blossom with dark leaves, are set around the rim. The teapot collar carries part of the border design.

A large flower filled urn sits upon a tall pedestal in the center of the picture. Two pairs of young people sit at the base of the urn. Those at left read a book and there is a world globe at their feet. At left in the distance there is a sailboat. The children are nicely dressed and shod. The couple at right are in rags and there is a piece of chain near the boy's bare feet. In the distance there are a river, a building and some mountains. Perhaps this was meant as an allegory about the value of education.

Marked J.R. and Opaque China. GMK. 3253, c. 1830-41.

SOUVENIR (cont.)

SPANISH LADY

Probably mady by Thomas, John and Joseph Mayer

The edge of the mulberry saucer photographed is decorated with small dark fleur-de-lys. The upper third of the rim is covered with a fine net diaper design. Dark foliated scrolls flank flowers around the border and shadowy sprigs and ferns complete a wreath around the well.

The lady of the title is riding side-saddle away from the foreground. She is mounted on a white horse and she wears a short flaring cape and a very large brimmed hat decorated with flowers. She holds her falcon on her upraised hand. She is almost surrounded by a wreath of overscaled flowers. In the distance there are town buildings and mountains.

The coffee pot, printed in a dark pink, shows the lady on each side. The border design which is much enlarged appears upside down on the upper part of the pot and on the lid and the base. This pattern appears as UM14 (Unknown Miscellaneous Fourteen) in Book I page 733. (Laidecker states he saw this pattern marked (imp.) Mayer) c. 1843-55.

SPANISH LADY (cont.)

TEA PARTY

Made by Societé Ceramique

The white edge of the cup and saucer shown is enhanced by a narrow black band filled with stringing. The border design consists of stylized sunflowers, dark leaves with white veins, trailing stems, and crocus. The background is stippled. In the central scene a gentleman and a lady sit on a curved garden bench placed under a flowering tree. In front of them is a small round table with tripod legs. The table is covered with a white cloth and is set for tea, with pot, cream jug, and cups. A serving man stands in the left background. Behind him there is a balustrade. A tiny dog sits up and begs near the lady's feet. In the distance there are tall mountains. The cup shows the tea party group on one side, a shepherd on the other, and has a large stylized round flower in its bottom. This same pattern was made by William Smith in England c. 1825-30. The components of the design are the same but more realistic. This looks like a copy of the Smith work.

Marked Societé Ceramique, Maastricht.

"VAQUERO"

Made by Elsmore and Forster

The edge of this plate is decorated by a band of narrow foliated scrolls, set over fleur-de-lys, and placed in a dark ground. This is succeeded by a vine-like wreath. The same vine forms a frame around the medallion in the center, which contains a picture of a mounted horseman dressed in a hat with a plume, a bolero vest, and wide-flared decorated trousers. He is holding a lasso in his right hand and has caught and felled a large wild horse which flounders in the foreground. The edge border of this plate and the cowboy scene are printed in tan lustre.

Marked as above (imp.) in a circle with Tunstall. GMK. 1476, 1853-71.

WATER GIRL
Made by James & Ralph Clews

This saucer is printed in cobalt and the edge is outlined by a narrow wavy white line. The border design consists of scallop shells alternating with a trio of flowers that are confined by curved scrolls.

The central scene shows the girl of the title standing near a well. She wears a cap and a dark dress, is barefoot and rests a large jug on the brick ledge of the well. A small dog and a barrel are near her at left. Laidecker named this pattern.

Marked (imp.) Clews Warranted Staffordshire, GMK. 919, 1818-34.

Juvenile Category

AMUSEMENTS
Maker Unknown

The stippled rim of this sauce dish is covered with a wreath of stylized daisies and large leaves. The white outer edge is decorated with a band of scallops and beads and the well is separated from the stippled rim by scallops and a beaded spearpoint design. In the center scene three children play on a grassy bank. One is seated and peers through a telescope, one holds a bubble pipe and the third, in the foreground, dances as he holds a balloon.

BOWER (THE)

Made by Edge, Malkin and Co.

The child's plate shown has a border design on the upper rim of rectangles and triangles. The triangles form an arched wreath around the central scene of a little girl who sits in the bower of the title. She wears a very large hat with a huge plume and she pats the spaniel seated at her knee. There are over-scaled flowers at right.

Marked *E.M. & Co., GMK. 1442, dated 1871-1903.*

"BY THE RIVER"

Made by Davenport

The edges of these toy plates are outlined by a fine beaded line. The upper part of the rim is dark and stippled. Small white crosses separated by two white beads are contained by white scrolls at the cavetto. In the center of the plate a man with a hat and cane escorts a woman wearing a shawl and hat and carrying a parasol. They are in the foreground on the bank of a river. A large sailboat is at left, and across the stream there are a house, a tower, and a bushy high bank. A spray of five-petalled flowers is in the foreground and runs up the right side. The plate is printed in black.

The scene shown on the platter shows the river in the center with a large sailboat pulled up to shore. A man with a top hat talks to a seated friend on the bank in the foreground. At right there are flowers and at left there are tall elms and more flowers. In the distance across the stream there are a mansion, arched bridge, trees and distant mountains. The platter is blue and white.

Marked (imp.) as above with an anchor, GMK. 111A, dated 1856.

CAPITOL AT WASHINGTON (THE)

This is an Alphabet plate and its outer edge is detailed with a band of reddish purple lustre and an embossed band of small hooks placed over the raised letters of the alphabet.

In the center the capitol of the United States is pictured. A pair of goats recline in the foreground. There are other goats under a tree in the left background. Women in long gowns with bustles are paired with gentlemen in dark jackets, light trousers and tall hats. They stroll near the building and on its steps.

DIMITY

Probably made by Charles Meigh

The ten-sided plate shown has a border pattern of white ovals and scrolls. The upper part of the rim is dark and stippled. The lower part of the rim is covered with narrow horizontal lines. A band of narrow wave-like scallops contains the border pattern. The rest of the plate is covered with a design of stars and beads. These dishes have been recorded in green and in brown.

The mark is probably GMK. 2618, used from 1835-1849.

DOG IN THE MANGER, THE

The upper rim of this alphabet plate is decorated with a beaded, dark outer band, a row of arch forms and a third band of diamonds. The rest of the rim is covered with the letters of the alphabet. The top of the well bears the title "Aesop's Fables." The bottom, "Dog In The Manger." Pictured is a small terrier snarling and yapping at three hungry horses. He is lying in their bed of hay and he will not allow them access to it although he, himself, has no use for it.

"FIRST STEPS"

Made by John Rogers & Sons

A narrow dark band encircles the edge of this little dish. The rim is embossed with a wreath of palmettos. In the center scene a small child walks toward a seated woman as he grasps her hand.

Marked (imp.) Rogers, GMK. 3369, c. 1814-36.

JUNGLE SCENE

Maker unknown

A small black boy dressed in a white suit and vest is fleeing from a very large tiger who emerges from its lair in the center of the scene. The rim of the plate is embossed with scrolls that form ovals which contain embossed birds.

LITTLE GIRLS PLAYING BALL

Probably made by Enoch Wood & Sons

The edge of this cup plate is trimmed with a narrow henna red band. The scene in the center of the two girls is also printed in henna and is framed in the well by an octagon.

Marked (imp.) Wood and "N" GMK. 4247, 1818-46.

MY PLAY FELLOW

Maker unknown

Here are four items from a set of children's dishes. The title appears at the base of the center scene which shows a little girl kneeling in a garden and playing with her kitten that is seated on a small pedestal table. The cream pitcher has a different picture and shows at left the little girl gardening. All other items noted to date have borne the picture of child and cat. One plate has a border design hand painted in many colors. The rest are bordered with a simple band of black at the edge and a narrow black band on the upper rim and some also include a pink lustre border. The scene is printed in a greyish-black.

MY PLAY FELLOW (cont.)

ROBINSON CRUSOE

In the center of this dish the name Robinson Crusoe is placed above the picture of that man as he poles a raft down a jungle river.

Godden shows this exact mold on page 247 in his "British Pottery" and attributes it to Bailey and Ball c. 1847-50.

Polychrome Chinoiserie with Lustre

FORMOSA *Made by Petrus Regout. This pattern appears in Book I, page 586 and that plate is backstamped "Slamat". Perhaps this bowl was part of a re-issue.*

"GARDEN SCENE" *(cream pitcher) Made by Hillditch & Son. Picture of a Mandarin dressed in dotted robe, seated under a canopy. Marked H. & S. Exact GMK. 2027, 1822-30.*

JAPAN *Made by Hancock, Whittingham & Co. The edge of the saucer shown is decorated with a band of fretwork containing four oval reserves which show a rock form at right and a large peony at left.*

A large two storied temple placed on a platform is in the center of the central scene. It has curved ornate rooves from which large bells hang from the corners. A tall epi crowns the top roof. There is a fence which crosses the foreground and at left one sees two junks under fill sail. A small island containing a temple is at upper left, and there are rocks and a peony tree at upper right. In the foreground there are the same rocks and overscaled peonies that appear in the border reserves.

Marked H.W. & Co., GMK. 1936, c. 1863-72.

"LADY WITH BIRD IN HAND" *(small saucer 4⅜") Unmarked.*

323

"MAN WITH BIRD" *(sauce boat) Made by James & Ralph Clews. Man seated in garden holds a pole. Bird on tree branch near a hanging ornament.*

Marked (imp.) CLEWS, 1818-34. Mark not located.

TAMURLANE *(plate) Marked (ptd.) J. & M.P. Bell & Co. Also marked (imp.) J.B. and a bell. GMK. 317-318. This dish was made in Scotland. It displays the same picture transfer as the Timor patterns made in Holland, France and Germany. (See Book I pages 591 and 592.)*

Tamerlane (1336?-1405), a descendant of Ghenghkis Khan was an oriental Mongolian who was also known as Timur Lenk, or Timur the Lame. His conquests extended from his city of Samarkand into Northern India, Turkey and Egypt in Asia Minor, and ranged from the Persian Gulf to the Volga River, and from the Hellespont the the Ganges. His name was known and feared everywhere. Here then is possibly the explanation for the fact that many potters from different European countries used the name Timor for the same Oriental design. The story behind the picture has yet to be revealed.

TEA SERVICE ON CARPET *(saucer 5")* *Unmarked.*

WOODSEAT *(hot water dish) Made by Minton. Good luck symbols in the border. Tall vase in center. Marked (imp.) Minton and B.B., GMK. 2695, dated 1866.*

Miscellaneous Category

AFRICANA
Made by Edward and George Phillips

The scalloped edge of this pink dish is trimmed with a lacy band of beads from which tear-shaped short pendants descend towards the well. In the reserves formed by the teardrops there are three scenes of a goddess in a fancy boat pulled by swans. Three pairs of large flowers alternate with the scene. The two designs are separated by a shell and floral bouquet. Sprigs and flowerettes from every part of the rim design enter the cavetto.

Two large smiling lions, one recumbent and one standing on a rock are placed in the flower strewn foreground of the central scene. In the background there is a mansion, a stream meanders behind the beasts and tall trees rise from its banks.

Marked E. & G. P., GMK. 3008A, 1822-34.

AMERICAN LARK (THE)

Maker Unknown

A band of small spearpoint surrounds the stippled upper rim of this lavender saucer. Three passion flowers, leaves and scrolls alternate with dahlias and a lily, leaves and a scroll in the lower border.

The bird of the title is perched upon a large blossom at right. Other overscaled flowers are placed across the foreground and a dahlia grows up and curves over the lark's head at left.

ANTELOPE
Made by Job and John Jackson

The upper rim of the scalloped saucer shown is covered with a diamond diaper pattern. The border is divided into three dark and three light areas. The three floral areas are made dark by a fine net. The light areas, left white, are crowned by four arch forms. The area under the arches is filled with long pendants of leaves and beads.

The central picture of a young girl feeding a bridled antelope is surrounded by a wreath of cartridge forms filled with vertical sprigs set on a large bead.

Marked Jackson's Warranted, GMK. 2156, 1831-5.

BEEHIVE

Probably made by William Ridgway & Co.

The outer edge of this dish is decorated with a band of small dark pennants. Six baroque forms framed by scrolls and filled with a lattice design separate six pairs of large flowers placed in a diaper design of small rosettes. The sprigs and leaves from the flowers cross the cavetto.

The beehive of the title is in the left foreground. It is situated on a grassy flower-strewn river bank and is surrounded by flowers, sprigs and leaves. A fanciful tree rises at left behind the hive. Across the stream there is a flower filled urn set upon a table. Two pointed mountain peaks are seen in the background.

Like GMK. 3303A, 1834-54.

BIRDCAGE

Maker Unknown

The pattern on the outside of this blue and white bowl is repeated in a smaller scale on the upper part of the inside rim. Vertical curved beaded lines cover the background of this portion of the pattern. A band of small quatrefoils crosses the middle of the wavy lines and sprays of flowers are placed on the band. The top edge of the design is trimmed with a wreath of dark oval beads. The birdcage of the title appears in the bottom of the dish.

BIRDCAGE (cont.)

DETAIL

"BLUE AND WHITE SHEET PATTERN"

Made by James and Ralph Clews

The entire surface of this miniature plate (3") is covered with a bold design of stylized plant forms which appears to be geometric.

Marked (imp.) Clews and a crown. Mark not located, but it is similar to GMK. 918, 1818-34.

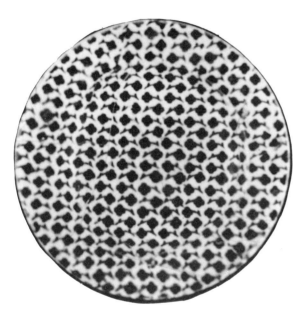

BOUQUET

Mark not located

The body of this creamer is covered with an alternating design of pinwheel-shaped stylized flowers and a square cross composed of furled leaf shapes centered with a white Gothic cross design. Dark scrolls are placed over the floral pattern and under the cross designs. Small foliated scrolls surround each design element. A band of dark scalloped beads surround both the top part of the body and the outer edge. The trim around the collar echos that used in the body.

Marked JJJ.

337

BRITISH BIRDS
Made by Samuel Alcock & Co.

There is a band of tiny laurel leaves around the edge of this dish. The rim is covered with a wreath of clumps of apple blossoms, buds, leaves, and small ferns.

In the center a lark perches on a twig at right over a large nest containing eggs. Oak leaves, apple blossoms, sprigs, and ferns spread across the foreground.

Marked S. A. & Co., GMK. 75, 1830-59, dated 1855.

BRITISH TAMBOURINE

Made by Mellor, Venables, & Co.

The edge of this plate is decorated with a wreath of ovals and beads. The upper part of the rim is covered with a design of beaded slanted vertical lines which give the effect of lacy swags. Flowers are placed at the bottom of each swag.

In the center a bird perches on a branch of a lotus tree next to a tree branch of overscaled flowers. There is a butterfly above the bird.

Marked (imp.) as above, GMK, 2646, 1834-51.

CAMDEN

Possibly made by John Ridgway

A wreath of diamonds set over a stippled background decorates the edge of this saucer which is printed in a medium light blue. The border design consists of small round beads surrounded by straight rays which give a diamond diaper effect. A band of the small diamonds contain the border at the cavetto and a delicate spearpoint enters the well.

A wreath of dainty flowers frames the central ten-pointed star centered with a bead, circle of rosettes and triangular rays.

Marked with a royal coat of arms, GMK. 3258, 1841-55. (See SOUVENIR, [Floral Category] this book for same mark.)

CARROLL

Made by Samuel Alcock & Co.

This plate is twelve sided and the upper part of the concave panelled rim is covered in a very dark blackish blue. A series of single large shaggy petalled flowers and large leaves are separated by foliated scrolls that descend to the well. Three of these scrolls terminate in shamrocks.

The central medallion is composed of the scrolls of flowers radiating from a dark central area.

Marked S. A. & Co., GMK. 75, 1830-59.

CHINESE BIRDS
Made by Davenport

The floral framed reserves in the border pattern on this mulberry dish contain a scene of a classic temple-like building in the center background. At right there is a dark sailboat and at left a pair of dark elms. The reserves are separated by scrolls that form ovals with dark centers inset with a white rosette. Flowers and leaves are placed between the two design elements.

In the center scene the long tailed, crested birds of the title are perched on the branches of a slender tree which is placed upon a pedestal. A curved bridge with railings composed of scrolls crosses a stream at right. In the left foreground there is a pair of overscaled flowers.

Marked as above, printed name like GMK. 1187, 1820-60.

CORAL

Possibly made by Jacob Furnival

The border design on this ten sided dish consists of vertical branches of alternating light and dark coral strands. The outer edge is embossed. A group of seashells, seaweed and coral branches is placed in the center. Marked J. F. (if Furnival, 1845-70).

CORINTH
Made by Wedgwood

A border design of Greek stylized palmetto leaves surrounds the upper half of the rim of this plate. The same leaves form a fan design around a star and form a six petalled stylized flower in the center of the dish.

Marked (imp.) as above also (imp.) Wedgwood Pearl, GMK. 4075 and 76, c. 1840-68.

COTERIE

Made by John Ridgway

The rim of this dish is covered with a field of stylized small three petalled flowers on straight stems. The border is contained at the top and the bottom by a band of white oval beads, and a further band of narrow hairpin arches surrounds the well. In the center a circle of the flowers surrounds a single blossom. This plate is printed in pale blue.

Marked (imp.) as above, GMK. 3254, 1830-41.

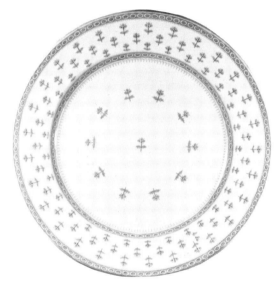

"CUPID IMPRISONED"

Made by Enoch Wood and Sons

    This deep saucer is printed in cobalt. The edge is detailed by a band of links. The Cupid of the title is placed behind bars in the center; he holds his hand outstretched to the viewer. A border design of very large flowers surrounds the scene. There is no title backstamp on the dish. Laidecker recorded the pattern with the above name.

    Marked (imp.) Wood, GMK. 4247, c. 1820-30.

DENTELLE

Probably made by Boch Freres

This small bowl presents a design of fans and rosettes set over arches of fleurons with a diamond pendant in the center. The upper part of the bowl is dark and is stippled and is contained at the top by a band of white beads. In the center bottom of the bowl there is a circular design composed of the rosettes. Dentelle is the french word for lace work.

Marked B. F., may be Boch Freres, Belgium, c. 1850.

DIAMOND PATTERN
Maker Unknown

The edge of this unevenly scalloped dish is white. The concave rim is covered with a design of diamonds centered with quatrefoils connected with small crosses set against a background of beaded rays. The border pattern crosses the cavetto and is contained in the well by a band of small dark diamonds and tiny outward pointing arrows.

In the central design long sprawling dahlias, sprays, sprigs and dark leaves are placed around the well. A curved piece of trellis ending in a pillar of diamond pattern trellis forms a background for the floral bouquets.

EAGLE

Made by Ralph Hall

The border pattern on this saucer consists of scallop shell shapes flanked by dolphins that alternate with double foliated scrolls. These are set against a dark stippled background. The central picture occupies the rest of the saucer and consists of a large eagle, wings outspread, which is riding a curved boat filled with arrows and flags. There are sea waves in the foreground and in the background one can faintly see towered buildings. Clouds complete the circular picture. This is another example of historical china made for the American trade but is included in this book because of the interesting transfer picture.

Marked R. Hall and Sons, GMK. 1889, c. 1836.

EAGLE (cont.)

EAST KENT YEOMANRY SALT DISH
Made by Spode

A band of diamonds is placed around the top of this salt dish. The motto and the coat of arms of the title is on one side. It is flanked by dark flowers at left, and white flowers set in a stippled field at right. The other side of the vessel carries the picture of a large dark rose.

Marked Spode and New Fayence. Exact GMK. 3655, c. 1805-33.

EASTERN PLANTS

Made by James Edwards

The entire face of the gently scalloped toddy plate is covered with a design of vertical wallpaper stripe type. The white areas contain vertical sprays of flowers. The dark stippled areas are centered with a design of four pendants topped by a pair of roses. A wreath of small scallops and spearpoint contains the border pattern in the well and encircles a clear center circle.

The second dish shows the wallpaper border and the center does carry a scene of an overscaled flower at left center and a man on a camel in the middle right distance. In the far distance one sees a lake and a tall pointed mountain.

Marked J. E., GMK. 1449, 1847-51.

FAIRY

Made by Ralph Cochran & Co.

The panelled rim of the saucer shown is covered with concentric narrow lines. Three small scenic oval reserves show a dark urn at right, a tower in the background and a tree at left. The reserves are separated by pairs of large flowers. A wreath of white beads contains the border pattern at the well.

In the center scene four girls dance in the right foreground. They are near a balustrade topped with urns filled with flowers. A tall elm rises behind the balustrade. A river divides the scene and there are domed buildings and a tall slender tower at left in the background and a small boat afloat midstream.

Marked R. C. & Co., GMK. 965, 1846 plus.

FAIRY QUEEN
Made by William Ridgway & Co.

A band of small diamonds is placed around the dark edge of this pitcher, and a succeeding band of stippled ovals is transversed by a pair of narrow white lines. Dark triangular patterns set in foliated scrolls are interspersed in the band. Flowers and sprigs are set on the lower part of the collar.

The fairy queen of the title is carried in a plumed chariot by a pair of large peacocks. There are overscaled flowers placed at either side of the picture. Behind the queen one sees a river and an island on which there is a small domed temple.

Marked W. R. & Co., GMK. 3303A, 1834-54.

FEATHER
Made by Ralph Hall & Co.

The center of this fourteen sided plate is covered with three large swirling feathers and flowers. The feathers have eyes that resemble peacock feathers. Three stylized rosettes are placed around the feathers. A smaller version of the design is placed in five spots around the concave panelled rim.

Marked R. H. & Co., GMK. 1890A, 1841-9.

"FEATHER FLOWERS"

Made by Ridgway & Morley

This plate is sixteen sided and the rim is panelled. The design of three sprays of white centered flowers surrounded by feather sprigs is printed in mulberry over painted with green, gold and blue and alternates with three single blossoms of the same type. The central flower consists of a green blossom, a bright blue leaf shape and mulberry sprigs sprays and flowerettes.

Marked as above and "Improved Granite China" Mark not listed. 1842-44.

FERN

Possibly made by Samuel Alcock

The rim of this cup plate is covered with a wreath of small dark flowers and delicate fern fronds. The same two elements are used in the center medallion. A variation on this pattern is shown in Book I on page 626 and that dish was made by John and George Alcock.

Marked (imp.) with a beehive and Alcock. See note in Godden re: GMKs 75, 76, 77, 1830-51.

357

FLORENTINE FOUNTAIN
Made by Davenport

A wreath of rosettes alternating with a stylized leaf design is placed around the dark edge of this unevenly scalloped dish. The indented rim is stippled and carries a design of a large white butterfly perched in the center of a flowering branch, and a dark butterfly sitting on a flower flanked by dark leaves. The border pattern covers the cavetto and invades the well. It is contained by a string of white beads which holds tiny quatrefoils. A second narrow band of tiny sprigs that resemble fleur-de-lis surrounds the central scene.

The tall fountain in the center of one dish is supported by a pair of dolphins which in turn support the top base. A scalloped shell decorates the pedestal. Flowers and sprigs are placed on either side of the fountain and form a circular background. The scenes on the dishes differ as seen on the second dish photographed. The border is the distinguishing design element.

Marked as above (imp.) and (ptd.) GMK. 1181A, c. 1830-35.

FLORENTINE FOUNTAIN (cont.)

FOREST

Made by Joseph Clementson

This pattern is shown in Book I on page 630 and was attributed to Samuel Alcock. Here is a cup and saucer printed in sepia. The pattern was also made by John Alleson, Seaham Potteries (Sunderland) 1838-41. Marked J. Clementson, GMK. 910A, c. 1839-64.

FRUIT & FESTOON

Maker Unknown.

Three cartouches containing fruit are set in a background of square basket weave on the border of this dish. Floral festoons are placed between the reserves. A band of snail-like scrolls frames the central picture of fruit, flowers and a butterfly.

"FRUIT AND WILD ROSE BORDER"

Made by Davenport

A band of white beads surrounds the slightly scalloped edge of this plate. The upper part of the border is very dark cobalt. Six large rounded fruits with leaves alternate with single wild rose blossoms suspended from rings around the concave rim. The fruit designs are flanked by scrolls that also hook into the rings.

In the central picture a large urn with thin snake handles is placed on the end of a brick wall. It is filled with a bouquet of large roses, poppies and tulip buds.

Marked (imp.) as above and with (imp.) anchor, GMK. 1181 c. 1805 plus.

GRECIAN BORDER

Made by Thomas Dimmock

The upper part of the rim of this scalloped dish is trimmed with large foliated scrolls interrupted at three points by a flame-like three-pointed leaf design. The lower rim and the cavetto are covered with a diaper design of small quatrefoils. A wreath of foliated scrolls contains the border design in the well.

The central medallion is a starburst design with twelve pointed rays surrounding a diaper field centered with a stylized rosette.

Marked D and Stoneware, resembles GMK. 1298, 1828-59.

HADDINGTON

Made by James and Ralph Clews

This small dish (3¼″) is printed in grey and shows a large shaggy ram standing on some grass and flanked by little sprigs. A wreath of grapevines, grapes and leaves covers the rim.

Marked (imp.) with a crown and Clews Warranted Staffordshire, GMK. 918, 1818-34.

"HUNTING DOG"

Made by James and Ralph Clews

This saucer is printed in cobalt and the edge is defined by a wreath of tight white scallops. The border design consists of a wreath of bold white foliated scrolls that form three reserves at the top and at the bottom of the rim. Those at the upper part contain a white flower set in a white circle and three small white dogwood-type flowers. In the lower arches the same white little flowers are set over a fine net pattern.

A white band encircles the central picture of the dog of the title. He wears a collar and stands with tail upraised as he looks over the bushes in the foreground into the meadows at right. Large rocks and a tree are in the background at left. There is a cottage in the right distance.

Marked (imp.) Clews Warranted Staffordshire and (ptd) "Stone China". GMK. 919, 1818-34.

HYDROGRAPHIC

Made by Davenport

The item photographed is a toothbrush box and we show one side of the dish with its medium blue transfer. The background is stippled and printed with wavy lines to simulate water. Small scrolls form medallions and are placed around the sides and contain pairs of birds drinking from a birdbath alternating with small bouquets. Hydro is a prefix denoting water; graphis comes from the Greek and means drawn or written, therefore, Hydrographic means "water look."

Marked as above, GMK. 1179A, 1820-60.

MADRAS

Made by Thomas G. Booth

The rim of this plate is decorated with a pattern that contains three reserves in which a water god holding a horn is driving a chariot pulled by dolphins with horse heads. These reserves are separated by cameo-like ovals that contain the profile of a woman. The designs are joined by a wreath of a narrow band of scrolls, and beads are placed over and under the band.

In the center scene a large lion with huge mane is set in a circle that contains tropical growth that resembles bamboo. Madras is in India. This pattern is late but is presented because of the amusing classical border and primitive center.

Marked T. C. B., it is like mark 449, the pattern was registered in 1872.

MAYFIELD

Maker Unknown

The concave rim of this dish is covered with a design of coral-like twigs, branches, sunflowers and sprigs and a spray of pods. In the center a rococco basket form supports a large bouquet of assorted flowers, sprigs and leaves. None is realistic except for a dark tiger lily at top left.

ORNATE

Maker Unknown

The entire face of this scalloped dish with concave rim is covered with a closely intertwined pattern of shells, seaweed, sprigs and flowerets.

PARADISE

Made by John & George Alcock

This saucer is gently scalloped and the edge is detailed with a row of beads. It is printed in green and the upper part of the rim is covered with lacy swags that enclose pairs of small flowers. The lower rim is stippled. A wreath of rosettes, beads and sprigs frame the central medallion which shows a pair of exotic birds on a terrace. There is a large flower-filled urn on a pedestal at right. In the distance at left there are buildings and mountains and a lake.

Marked J.&G.A., GMK. 69A, 1839-46.

PAROQUET

Made by Ralph Stevenson

The outer edge of this saucer is detailed with a ribbon of small ovals connected by a dark line which is interspersed with a shell design at ten points. The upper stippled rim is contained by foliated rococo scrolls. Pairs of small flowers are placed over the scrolls. A narrow pointed fringe falls from the scrolls toward the center and four large single rose blossoms alternate with four large dahlia-types in the arches formed under the fringe. Each flower is flanked by tiny blossoms and sprigs.

The birds of the title are sitting facing each other on the branches of an elm that rises from a large jagged tree stump. Part of an elm tree grows from the stump and rises behind one of the birds at the upper right. There are sprigs and flowers in the foreground.

Marked R. Stevenson, GMK. 3704, 1810-34.

PEACOCK

Made by John Thompson

This plate is gently scalloped and the concave rim is covered with a design of white reserves separated by flowers, shell forms and sprigs set in a stippled ground. The reserves are framed by shell-like ruffles and feature a pair of birds seated on either side of a scrolled harp. The border design is confined by a wreath of shell-like scrolls and tassels which covers the cavetto.

In the center picture a large peacock sits on a platform placed on top of a pedestal composed of scrolls. A smaller bird perches at left. At right there is a fountain and at left one sees a river with a small boat and buildings on an island. In the foreground there is an overscaled rose at the foot of the pedestal.

Marked J. T., GMK. 3844, c. 1816-65.

PEACOCK

Maker Unknown

The rim of the saucer photographed is covered with a pattern of beaded white lace-like stripes that curve to the left. Single large blossoms with leaves and small pendent bunches of grapes are placed over the background design. At the upper edge small dark spade shapes and sprigs flanked by scrolls are placed between the flowers. The border is contained at the bottom by a wreath of bell forms.

The peacock of the title perches on a fence at left. At right there is a four-sided scrolled pedestal on which a flower filled urn is seen. An elm rises at center and there is a fence between the pedestal and the peacock which is composed of diamond cutouts.

PERSIAN BIRD

Made by Davenport

The upper part of the rim of this scalloped plate is decorated with a wreath of foliated scrolls against a dark upper field of a wavy diaper design. Small sprigs are placed under the scrolls.

A frame of triangular leaf shapes is placed around the central transfer that shows two exotic birds, one in flight and one wading. A butterfly is placed at upper right and a large overscaled flowering tree with large leaves and berries is in the left foreground. This dish is printed in multicolor, it was also made in Flow Blue.

Marked as above, GMK. 1187, c. 1852.

PERSIANS

Maker Unknown

The edges of these dishes are defined by a band of tiny quatrefoils and crosses. The stippled border, covered with white beaded crosses, is inset with three scrolled reserves containing fruit. A double scroll that forms an oval opening separates the reserves. Beneath each reserve there is a stylized acanthus.

On the small plate, which is backstamped, a woman in Grecian dress holds a saucer to obtain water from a fountain that rises above a pedestal basin. The large plate, which is not backstamped, may be from a different pattern series as it contains no human figures. A large bird with double tail is perched above a cluster of fruits and flowers. Note that the fruit in the rim reserves are different on each plate. The saucer reserves are filled with grapes. Those on the larger plate picture a basket of a fruit mix of gooseberries, cherries and flowers.

Marked B.

PERSIANS (cont.)

"PINK PEONIES"

Probably made by John Rogers and Son

The edge of this plate is encircled with large beads. The entire background is stippled and large white peony-type flowers and large dark stylized leaves with white veins cover the dish. The dish is printed in pink.
Marked (imp.) Rogers, GMK. 3369, c. 1800-36.

RAILWAY

Made by Beardmore and Edwards

This jug has a rim pattern of square beads centered with quatrefoils set over a base of beaded pennants terminating in fleur-de-lis. The railway engine shown bears the name "Express." There are no figures on the coal car nor in the open carriage at the end, but passengers can be seen in the two fancy carriages in the center. Printed in black with colour added on details.

Marked B. & E., GMK. 306, 1856-8.

RIBBON WREATH
Made by Minton

A narrow band of orange lustre is placed around the edge of this dish. A small band of beads and crosses is next to the edge lines. The wreath of the title is placed around the rim. A small circle of flowers and sprigs is placed in the center of the dish. The printing is multi-coloured.

Marked M. and Co., and (imp.) Minton BB, Dated November 12, 1851.

SEA FAN

Made by John Wedgwood

A wreath of beaded sea fronds covers the rim of this pink and white saucer and the sprays from these extend far into the well. In the center a fan shaped shell is surrounded by small sprigs of seaweed.

Marked (imp.) W. W. and (ptd.) J. Wedgwood, GMK. 4276 and 4276A, 1841-60.

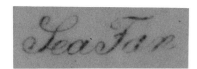

SEASONS (THE)

Made by Copeland

We show two pale blue dishes in this pattern. The unevenly scalloped soup plate has an outer edge of C-scrolls and small vase forms. The rim design consists of four oval cartouches that picture cherubs in the garb of the four seasons. The vignettes are separated by horizontal lines and filled with a diaper design of quatrefoils. A band of thick scrolls is placed under the rim and forms a quatrefoil frame for the center scene of a large urn filled with overscaled summer flowers. In the background there is a river and a triple-arched bridge, city buildings on either bank and a few poplar trees. A large spotted lily is placed in the foreground at the pedestal of the vase.

The second dish, of course, carries the same border design. In the center scene an ornate urn filled with a large bouquet is placed at the top of some steps in the foreground. It appears to be on a terrace as there is a balustrade at left. In the background one sees a formal garden with fountains and urns and in the distance there are trees and hillsides.

These dishes are reissues of the pattern made by Copeland and Garrett 1833-47. Marked Copeland (imp.) over a crown, like GMK. 1072, c. 1900.

SPIRAL

Made by W. Baker & Co.

This plate is twelve sided and the panelled rim is stippled at top. A wreath of white feathery leaves is placed against the dark upper band. Five large stylized and over painted flowers are set around the rim and there are pairs of smaller flowers between them. Sprays enter the well from the large flowers and the design in the center is composed of three swirling sprigs.

Marked as above, GMK. 230, 1860 plus.

SWISS HARP

Made by Francis Dillon

This saucer is printed in black and the edge is outlined by a line of small scallops. The upper rim is covered with a stippled band with foliated scrolls which form swags in three sections and enclose black triangular flower filled designs in the alternate sections. Large single open roses with black leaves alternate with trios of asters around the lower rim.

In the center of the dish a maiden in a white empire gown sits on a high stippled bank and plays the harp of the title. Her bonnet is on the ground beside her and the bank is strewn with flowers. At left a scroll framed cartouche containing a scene of a river, an ornate sailboat and high peaked mountains is placed over a wall composed of black squares. The same scrolls enclose the space over the girl and her harp.

Marked (imp.) Dillon, GMK. 1288, 1834-43.

TUSCAN SPRIG

Maker Unknown

A narrow band of small loops encircles the edge of this saucer. A wreath of foliated scrolls and rosettes is set against a dark background in the upper part of the border. Four trios of serrated leaves are placed around the rim and the spaces between them are filled with sprays of flowerettes. This plate is printed in sepia. The sprig of the title appears in the center with sprays of the flowerettes. A circle of small cornucopias filled with large asters, flowerets and leaves surrounds the central sprig.

VINE
Made by Wedgwood

A narrow band of inverted hearts and darts is placed around the outer edge of this lavender and white dish. The slightly concave rim is covered with a wreath of grapevines, grapes, leaves and flowerets. In the center there is a large open blossom with leaves and tendrils.

Marked (imp.) Wedgwood Pearl, like GMK. 4086, c. 1840-68.

WASHINGTON

Maker Unknown

Three different vignettes are set into the stippled sepia border of this saucer. One shows a sailboat with a single dark sail at right and a castle at left across the river, the second shows a towered castle set upon a five arched foundation and the third also contains a boat with double white sails at right. The vignettes alternate with shield shapes composed of foliated scrolls. The outer edge is detailed with a band of dark scallops and fleur-de-lis and dark sprigs are placed between the shields and vignettes.

S-scrolls frame the central scene which shows a woman representing Fame placing a circlet over the head of the large bust of George Washington. At left there is a part of a balustrade and in the distance there are a river and a small castle, and in the far distance one sees two small mountain peaks.

WOOSTER COUNTY AGRICULTURAL SOCIETY

This dish has no border decoration at all and in the center framed by a cartouche wreath of wheat, corn and flowers is the name of the society and its date of chartering.

Unascribed Patterns

Unascribed Patterns

The dishes shown in this section have no backstamps nor any other identification, and therefore cannot be attributed in this book. So that more may be learned about their origins, they are presented here with an abbreviated description of each item. The pattern names and/or makers may be forthcoming from further study and research, and will be published in future corrections of this book. The author welcomes assistance by collectors, students and experts.

In order to facilitate correspondence it was necessary in the first book to formulate a list and assign a code number and letter to each design. This list follows the format of the first book. The letter "U" means unascribed, and precedes a letter denoting type such as "G" for Genre or "S" for Scenic. In this book we added the letter "S" in front of the letters that denote the pattern number. In other words, we will say Supplemental Unknown Scenic I so you would have S.U.S. I, or if it was an oriental pattern it would say Supplemental Unknown O, i.e., S.U.O. The word ascribe means to credit in writing or speech, let us hope that the words will be forthcoming so these patterns can be ascribed in the future.

S.U.F. #1. *Pierced fruit basket, blue and white with central picture of melon, grapes and sprigs, floral border.*

S.U.F. #2. *Master salt. Black and white. Diameter three inches. Height 2¼ inches. Scrolled border. Large dahlia in the center of the body.*

S.U.F. #3. *Pair of violet printed cup plates with scrolled border and floral pattern variation in the center.*

S.U.F. #4. *Cup plate. Printed in green with a narrow border wreath of leaves and berries. Center scene of bird sitting on basin flanked with sprays of roses, thistles and shamrocks, the symbols of Great Britain.*

S.U.F. #5. *A band of quatrefoils placed over large blossoms separated by vertical bars containing quatrefoils. The center medallion, a bouquet encircled by Gothic key-hole scrolls.*

S.U.F. #6. *Tea pot. Pale blue and white. Roses set into narrow vertical swirling lines.*

S.U.F. #7. *Pair of pale blue toy plates (4½ inches). Rope edge. Concave rim. Central pattern of exotic birds, peonies and roses.*

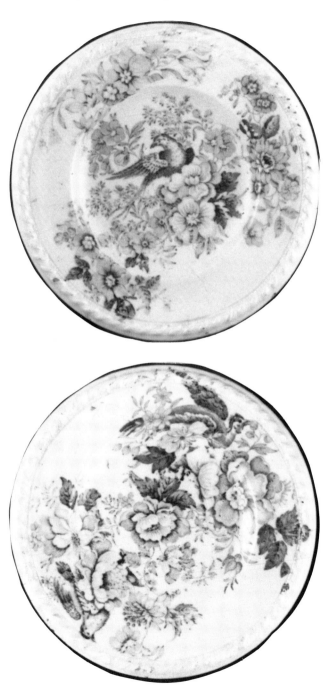

S.U.F. #8. *Hot water dish. Printed in light red and white. Beaded shields alternate with roses flanked by dark white-veined leaves in the border.*

S.U.F. #9. *Sepia and white platter. Gadroon edge. Bird in center on top of large dahlia. Another bird beneath the flower perching on scrolls. Flowers and sprigs on the lower rim.*

S.U.F. #10. *Red and white cup plate. Border of groups of hanging pods. Wild lilies in center.*

S.U.F. #11. *Blue and white cup plate. Top of border may be distinguishing mark with six triangular dark reserves flanked by scrolls. Flowers around the rim. Bird perched on bouquet in center.*

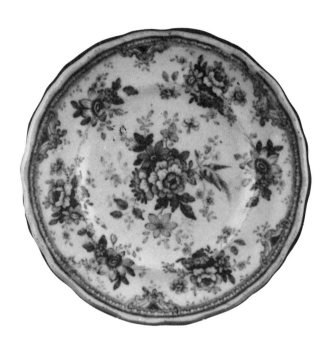

S.U.F. #12. *Red and white cup plate. Border of carnations and fruit (pears and small oval forms like nuts). The center scene of a bird perched on top of bouquet, oval fruit and nuts or buds at lower left.*

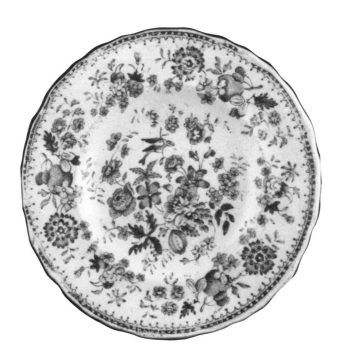

S.U.F. #13. *Blue and white dish. Entire dish covered with honeycomb diaper. Gothic arches against very dark ground around upper rim. Sprigs spray around central small basket with tall handle filled with bouquet.*

S.U.F. #14. *Cup plate with Gothic border design of pennants. A single long stemmed flower with fern-like leaves crosses the center of the dish which is printed in dark green.*

S.U.C. #1. *Sugar bowl with lion head handles. Border of diamond diaper pattern contained at top by a dark band interspersed with fleur-de-lis. Scene of statue of reclining woman and children set between pairs of large urns and vases. Columns and a wide arch in background.*

S.U.O. #1. *Vase in foreground on plate. Temples and pagoda in background. Border of scallops near edge and sprigs. The pattern is stylized green printing.*

S.U.O. #2. *Sepia printed cup plate. Border distinguished by stylized five-petalled flowers set in triangular reserves. Part of a man's head and spear alternating with flowers around the rim. Boat with many oars near tall temple with dome. Building may be mausoleum.*

S.U.O #3. *Cream pitcher. Printed in sepia with red accents. Chinese key and cloud motifs on collar. Willow story type detail in reserves on the side.*

S.U.O. #4. *Pale blue and white octagonal vegetable dish. Border of narrow concentric lines decorated with a wreath of oak leaves. Oriental boat with men in costume in foreground. Exotic trees. Pagoda with curved roofs in background.*

S.U.O. #5. *Cobalt platter. Scroll and floral border. Central scene of fountain at right. Tea house at center and pagoda in the background. Marked
(imp.) with a propeller. Might be Heath.*

S.U.O. #6. *Red and white bowl. Turban and scimitars separated by triangles in the border. Center scene of a Turkish archer.*

S.U.O. #7. *Tea pot. Mulberry. Reserves topped with a tent-like design. Flanked by bold white scrolls enclosing scene of two men in sheiks garb in foreground. Domed building on island in background with towers and minaret. Looks Arabian.*

S.U.O. #8. *Water pitcher. Border of flowers and scrolled diaper filled cartouches contained by acanthus leaves. Scene of five Arabs or Turks, the men in turbans, women in veils, looking at a bolt of cloth. Camel at left.*

S.U.S. #1. *Blue and white lobed dish. Stippled border of wild roses, tea roses and shadowy thistles and shamrocks, the Union Spray (the symbols of Great Britain), center of a cottage scene with a shepherd with lambs and a cow.*

S.U.S. #2. *Waste bowl. Blue and white. Dahlias in border. Scene on the side framed with scrolls of flowers and a pair of birds. Scene of a round building with conical roofs set upon an island.*

S.U.S. #3. *Border of lace-framed floral medallions. Center scene of a large piece of a corinthian column in the foreground. Many towered buildings in the left background. Small boat on river. Pale blue printing. Marked (imp.) British Porcelain.*

S.U.S. #4. *Pink and white printed scalloped dish. Large stylized flowers with two small exotic birds in the foreground. Sailboats in the middle ground.*

416

S.U.S. #5. *Border of flowers and sprigs on dish. Looks like Swiss patterns. Cottage in center resembles "Royal Cottage", (this book).*

S.U.S. #6. *Pitcher and basin. Blue and white with border of bold foliated scroll loops. Old farm house and many trees in pictorial transfer.*

S.U.S. #7. *Cup plate. Black and white. A dentil circle under the white embossed edge. Border of flowers at left. Center scene of a towered building with large columned entrance and steps down to river. Small dark boat on water and arched bridge in background.*

S.U.S. #8. *Gently scalloped dark blue and white dish. Border of eight vignettes separated by beaded vertical bands. Two vignettes show a pair of musicians on foot leading a sacrificial white bull, two others show seated shepherd with crook who plays on a horn to a fat sheep nearby, the third pair present a man kneeling before a seated figure with a sunburst emblem at left and the remaining two show a priest at left who holds a cross and appears to be blessing two horsemen. Central picture shows procession approaching gate. A man blowing a horn is leading two women who carry a basket and two men who carry pikes and escort a mounted horseman. A figure of victory is on top of the arch. There are church-like buildings at left.*

S.U.S. #9. *Cream pitcher. Blue and white. Worm track border with shell forms and buds at base. Center scene a standing guitar player and people kneeling at a shrine. A dark cross at left. Scene on reverse women kneeling at extreme left, the shrine and a tall white cross. Scene on the inside of the lip shows shrine and both crosses.*

S.U.S. #10. *Dish, printed in sepia, scalloped edge. Border print of Gothic arches separated by pairs of large blossoms. Central scene of large Gothic building framed by wreath of ribbon and flowers. Many small figures on street in foreground. Might be Copeland or Copeland & Garrett.*

S.U.S. #11. *Saucer gently lobed. Border of narrow vertical lines and six large flowers. A narrow string of diamonds around the center of the rim. Central scene framed by scrolls with tall dark monument at right. A building with two slender towers and a cupola in left background.*

S.U.S. #12. *Saucer printed in purple (or puce) with lustre edge. A cathedral or castle. Flag flying from its tower. A woman with sheep in a fenced enclosure in the foreground.*

S.U.S. #13. *Blue and white saucer with worm track border. Filled with flowerets. Central scene usual river picture with elms. A cottage at left. Woman sits on ground with baby in foreground. A man stands near her.*

S.U.S. #14. *Lobed dish. Black and white. A fountain scene with tall urn on pedestal in center. Man and woman stand nearby in court dress. Bold border pattern of fern fronds framing a temple and river scene divided by flowers and sprigs. A wreath of sprigs contains the pattern in well.*

S.U.S. #15. *Border background of narrow concentric lines. Scrolls separate five scenic reserves of castle flanked by trees. Border contained by wreath of scallops and pendent bells. Center scene of lake and a small cascade in foreground. Looks Tyrolean.*

S.U.S. #16. *Blue and white vegetable dish. Border of a vine connecting poppies, tendrils and leaves. Center scene of large Swiss chalet at left. A domed temple ruin at right. Man, woman and dog on the bank of a lake in the foreground.*

S.U.S. #17. *Cup plate. Black and white with an embossed edge. Shield reserves filled with dotted diamond diaper alternate with flowers. Background of narrow vertical lines. Six distinguishing black reserves with one half of a flower appear at the upper edge. Center scene of an English country house. Man and child on the driveway.*

S.U.S. #18. *Scalloped dish. Border with diamond diaper. Four large groups of flowers set over a petticoat pattern of scrolls. Center scene of an old arched bridge. Buildings at left. Small boat and standing man in foreground. The cup plate of this pattern is shown as U.S. 29 in Book I page 716.*

S.U.S. #19. *Border pattern of pendants and grapes set over a twining wave-like white band. Small center scene with castle at left high on a river bank. Tall plinth with urn in right foreground. Tall elm at right.*

S.U.S. #20. *Scalloped cup plate. Pink and white. Crenelated castle building at right. Church in left background. Tall trees that resemble those seen in "Canova".*

S.U.S. #21. *Coffee can. Diamond lozenge border inside top (not illustrated). Identical scene both sides. Large country house with lake in the foreground. Tall flower-filled white urn at left. Scene framed by tree branches.*

S.U.S. #22. *Pink and white cream pitcher. Stippled dotted border over bundles of fasces decorated with rosettes and separated by pairs of flowers. English scenery. The long bridge and country house is Compton Vernay. (This building was listed and pictured by Enoch Wood and identified as Compton Vernay Warwickshire.) The building on the reverse side is different.*

433

S.U.S. #23. *Pink and white tea pot. Border design of large various flowers set in sprigs. Scene on the side looks Swiss.*

S.U.S. #24. *Pink and white pepper pot or muffineer. A temple with Greek portico and an ornate tower next to a Gothic church structure. A river scene with flowers in the foreground on the reverse side.*

S.U.S. #25. *Concave rim. Blue and white dish. Rim covered with tiny dots that give a fine net effect and with foliated scrolls placed around it. Ruins of large Gothic church in background. Man with fishing rod, seated boy and dog on a high bank at left. River divides scene and rushes in small rapids between dark rocks in the foreground.*

S.U.S. #26. *Green and white cup plate. Border of rosettes. Italian scene in center. Tuscan mansion in right background. A tall arch at left. Man, lady and child in Renaissance costume in the center.*

S.U.S. #27. *Blue and white cup plate with fleur-de-lis edge. Basketweave background on border. Fleur-de-lis alternate with stylized roses with dark leaves around rim. Center scene of large mansion, lake or river and trees. Reg. mark dated Sept. 30, 1848.*

S.U.S. #28. *Blue and white cup plate. Edge of palmettos. Birds and flowers in border Center scene of a church ruin. Tall dark urn in the right foreground.*

S.U.S. #29. *Printed in light sepia. Bold border of sunflowers and large white scrolls. In the center a church at left looks Swiss. This pattern also is printed in green and white.*

S.U.S. #30. *Cup plate. Printed in dark sepia. Upper part of rim black. Scrolls and small flowers around the central scene of a barn-like structure and towered buildings in background. Tall trees on either side. Picture somewhat stylized. Looks Swiss.*

S.U.S. #31. *Cup plate, sepia and white. Border of trios of large blossoms separated by white scrolls. Central picture of rustic church.*

S.U.S. #32. *Trailing vines with rosettes set over concentric narrow lines filled with white beads is border design confined at well by a narrow vine. River scene in center. Men with fishing poles on bank at right. Two children and fallen log in center. Castles on both sides of river and a sailboat at left center. Blue and white.*

S.U.S. #33. *Water pitcher printed in pale blue. Border of basketweave and wreath of small shaggy dahlia-like flowers with leaves. Border design contained by beaded pennants. Central scene shows rustic garden house on elevation at left. Two women, a child and a man stand on a river bank at right. Large rock forms in foreground.*

S.U.S. #34. *Blue and white pitcher. Scrolls and shamrocks in stippled border. Vignettes in border show two rustic cottages. Lake or river scene on body. Row boat pulled up in foreground. Two men lean on boat. Tall trees at right. Many buildings on left bank. Probably Irish Scene.*

S.U.G. #1. *Geometric border with dahlias. Center scene on plate (illustrated) a girl with lamb. Printed in green and gold.*

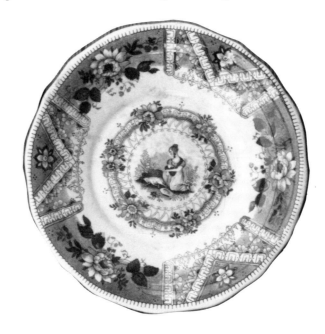

S.U.G. #2. *Plate with milk maid. Border of wild roses, tulips forget-me-nots and leaves. Center scene on the saucer has milkmaid standing near a cow and three lambs. Scene on cup (illustrated) shows a farmhouse in the background.*

S.U.G. #3. *Scene in the orient of occidental traders with high hats dealing with oriental merchants. Resembles Commerce, Book I, page 481. Marked (ptd.) H. Possibly Hackstaff. Sepia printing.*

S.U.G. #3 (cont.)

S.U.G. #4. *Hunting scene in dark cobalt. Rope edge. Morning-glories and sweet williams in border. Scene on the side of men fishing. Might be part of a Sporting series.*

S.U.G. #5. *Salmon fishing. Plate is scalloped. Edge is outlined with small dark cartridge forms. Six floral reserves alternate with shields around the border. There are dark leaves and specifically a passion flower in the lower right of the floral reserves. The central scene shows men fishing in rapids of a river. In the right background there are two small structures connected by a bridge and a waterfall rushes under the bridge. Printed in green.*

S.U.G. #6. *Scroll and floral border. Shepherd with crook. His dog behind him. Talks to a girl seated near a gushing spring. She holds a jug. Pink and white printing.*

S.U.G. #7. *Red and white cup and saucer. Border of twisted rope interspersed with roses and forget-me-nots. Four women with jugs, child and begging dog are pictured near a well. One side of the cup has the same scene, the other a woman who is feeding fowl stands near two children.*

S.U.G. #8. *Deep saucer, border stippled in sepia oval vignettes show a girl in long dress and big hat, who holds a chained bird, flower at left and a flower filled vase at right. Reserves separated by a lute, quiver and hunting horn. Center scene of Scottish hunter with rifle, kneeling on some rocks. A rushing stream in center. Deer fleeing on far bank. Tall trees and mountains in background.*

S.U.G. #9. *Dark blue & white plate. Upper part of rim is stippled and decorated with grapes and small flowers. Three large wing-like scrolls on the lower rim. Central scene of girl in long white dress asleep on grassy mound. At left, boy stands behind tree and watches her.*

S.U.M #1. *Green and white cup plate. Seaweed sprays centered with scallop shells and two pods. Look like sea fans.*

S.U.M #2. *Blue and white toy dish (3 inches). Bold border of white double C-scrolls set over a bead. Sheet pattern on body of white leaves, dark rosettes, and sprigs.*

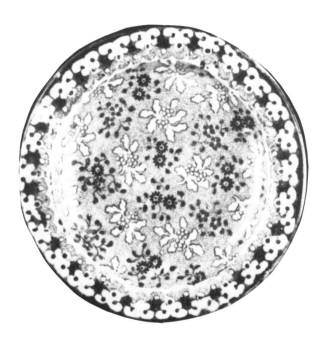

S.U.M. #3. *Black and white cup plate with large Chinese pheasant on branch of tree. Gothic tower on right bank of river. Many small boats on the river.*

S.U.M. #4. *Water pitcher. Mulberry and white. Border collar stippled background with a white scroll. Reserves shown contain flowers. Bird perched amidst overscaled flowers on the body. Marked (imp.) B.*

S.U.M. #5. *Cup plate. Stylized design of scattered feathers and groups of four leaf clovers and dark fern fronds. Background studded with tiny dotted rosettes. Multi-coloured.*

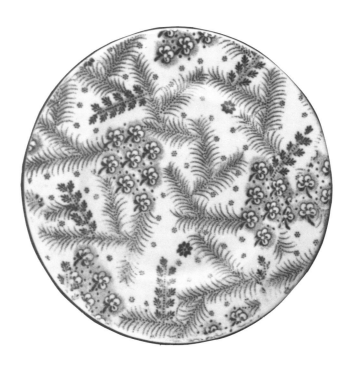

S.U.M. #6. *Cup plate. Multi-coloured. Thorns and flowers. Stylized forms, especially the thistles.*

S.U.M. #7. *Creamer. Collar pattern of vertical lines with a vine wreath. Bird perched on floral sprays in the center.*

S.U.M. #8. *Tea pot. Medium blue transfer. Pattern of sea urchins, conch shells and sprigs. Rose knob.*

S.U.M #9. *Cup plate. Blue and white. Scroll and flowers in border. Slanting vertical lines at the top. Bird perches in center of plate on top of large rounded fruits, flowers and nuts. Small flowers placed over the base.*

S.U.M. #10. *Green and white cup plate. Four sprigs of fern fronds centered with a pair of small flowers. A wreath of ivy in the center.*

S.U.M. #11. *Dish (5 inches). Bird at fountain. Border of dark grapes and leaves linked by vine. Exotic bird with crest perches on the rim of an ornate fountain basin. Palm trees at left. Section of oriental fence and overscaled flowers in the foreground. Printed in blue and white.*

S.U.M. #12. *Dish (9 inches). Sheet pattern of large white flowers on soft blue background.*

S.U.M. #13. *Dish (5½ inches). Lady with harp. Cobalt. Flowers and leaves in border. Large country mansion in left background.*

S.U.M. #14. *Tea pot. Stippled medium dark blue ground. Beaded circular medallions filled with small flowers on lid and upper rim. Acanthus sprays between medallions. Oval beaded reserves on each side with picture of small bird on a white sprig set over three overscaled peaches and other fruit. The same bird seen is on the top of the lid. The rest of the background is filled with forget-me-nots.*

S.U.M. #15. *Cup plate printed in light green. Border pattern of oriental birds perched on a branch with a mountain scene in distance. A small vase and sprigs are in the center.*

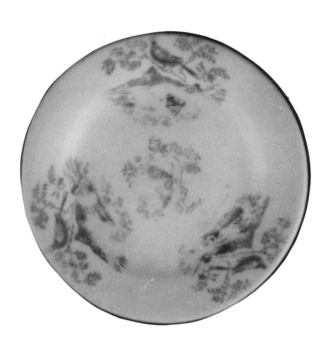

S.U.M. #16. *Blue and white cup plate with border of bold rosettes linked by sprigs. Central picture of a pair of Chinese pheasants perched on bits of trellis. Scene framed as medallion by a wreath of darts and ovals.*

PLATE IV

TRANSFER ART

TRANSFER DESIGNS ON PULLS

All the dishes shown in our books were printed in the early nineteenth century with the use of transfer papers pulled from copper plates. The potteries kept record books of their patterns by name, or number, or both, and with pulls. This section of the book is composed of a selection of pulls that were found, together with some drawings, in an old manual that turned up in New Jersey, U.S.A. They were part of a collection of papers that belonged to an artist named Victor Gallimore who worked in the Trenton potteries around 1910. Among the papers was a drawing manual presented as a prize to his father, William Gallimore, by the Wesleyan Day School in 1885 in Henley, England, and interspersed among the pages there were forty tissue paper transfer pulls, some stencils, and drawings of transfer patterns including a drawing of a border design signed E. Gallimore. A company with the name of Robert Gallimore is listed in Godden; its working years are indicated as 1831-40. It was located at St. James Place, Longton, and it was formerly known as A. & R. Gallimore The Robert Gallimore Company subsequently became Gallimore & Short-botham. Perhaps there is a link between these persons associated with the pottery business throughout the years.

Underglaze transfer printing on pottery was effected by the use of tissue paper proofs pulled from very thin rectangular copper plates. ($1\frac{1}{8}$th − 3 millimeters thick). The copper had been incised by an engraver with a design of his own or one adapted from a drawing or picture. The engravers usually free-lanced and sold their services to many potters as most manufacturers could not afford to employ their own engravers. The depth of the lines or dots that the engraver used determined the shades of the ink colours. Many designs were made in sets and the artist incised several copper plates with different elements of the design in order to fit properly on the various sized items in a set of dishes. The borders would vary in depth and the central scenes differed in more elaborate patterns.

The colour to be used was warmed, in order not to be too thick and was rubbed into the incisions of the design on the warmed copper plate; excess pigment was removed by a palette knife and the copper surface was wiped clean with a soft cloth called a boss. Special strong tissue papers cut to fit the size of the copper plate, were slightly dampened and placed over the copper surface and were pressed against it by an ordinary press. The resulting print was pulled from the plate and handed to a female transfer worker. The print that she held was in mirror image. She carefully placed the tissue face down on the bisque item to be decorated and rubbed it flat with a soft soapy flannel cloth. At this point the design appeared the same as that engraved on the copper plate. These women were responsible for placing the pattern in correct position on the bisque, joining the arcs of the border designs to form a circle without seams or overlap, putting bits of the design on cup handles, and on the handles and spouts of hollowware. They also cut the backstamp from the tissue and applied it on the underside of the dishes. The vessel was then dipped in water, the tissue floated off, the design and colour remained.

Not many copper plates are extant as they were thin, and copper is soft. They were used until the incised lines were worn down and the plates curved from the pressure of the roller presses. They had to be flattened out and repaired. Copper was very expensive and the plates were often melted down. A few plates can be seen in museums in England and in Scotland.

There are a few factory names on the pulls shown including that of Samuel Alcock & Co. on the Pompeii pattern, and with these we show a photograph of a dish printed with the pattern. The pictures of the pulls are reduced to fit the pages of this book. The old tissues are discoloured and fragile; we are surprised and delighted that they exist and that we can present them to our readers. The scenes are of course, romantic and fantastic. Perhaps some readers and scholars will be able to identify some of the patterns.

The pulls photographed in our book have been donated to the Margaret Woodbury Strong Museum in Rochester, New York, along with the transfer-decorated dishes that made up the Fountain House East collection. They will be exhibited there in the future.

POMPEII.
J & G. ALCOCK.

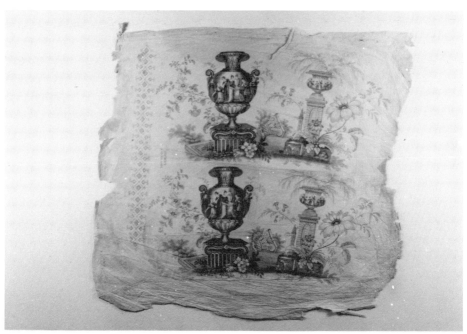

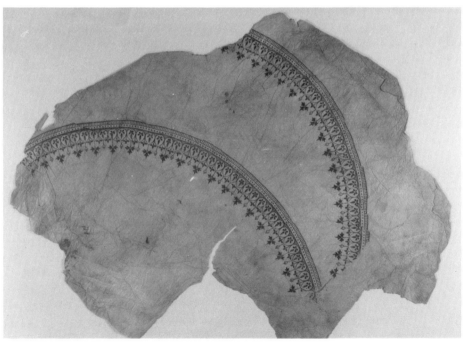

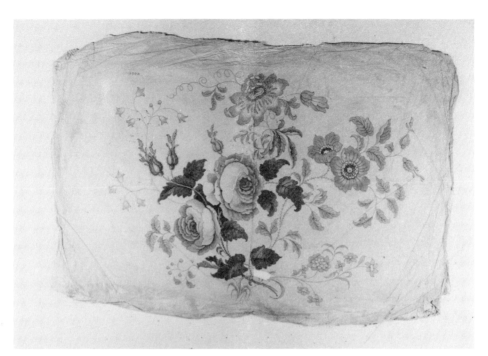

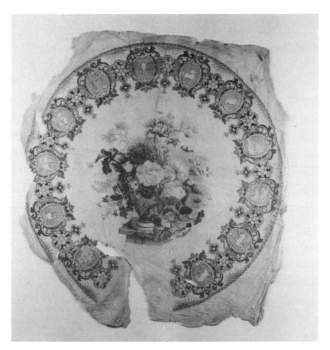

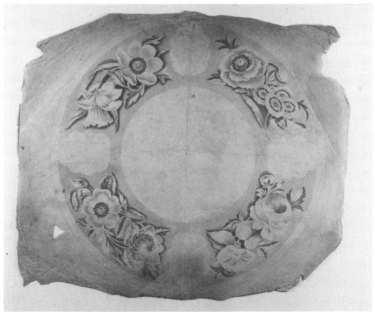

486

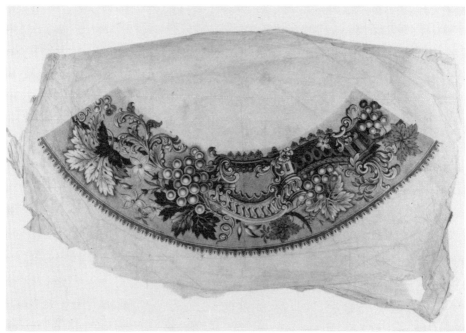

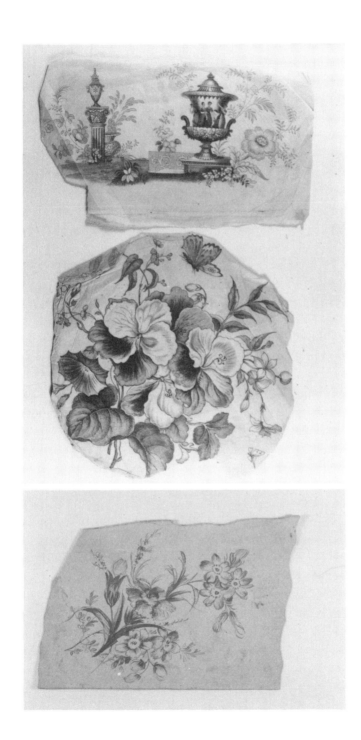

TYROL.
J. & G. ALCOCK.

Supplement To Book I

ADDENDA AND CORRECTIONS

Page 28   **ASIATIC PLANTS**

Shown here is a cup plate and a tea bowl. The flower strewn stippled border design includes wide triangular wing-like reserves containing a beaded diaper pattern. The large photograph of a green cup plate shows that the outer edge design of garlands has been omitted. A pale blue cup plate not illustrated used the pattern with garland intact but no inner band of stylized leaves, wavy circle, beads and quatrefoils.

The mulberry tea bowl carries the border design in its entirety and the swags at the rim are clearly shown.

The central floral designs differ on each size dish; the distinguishing feature would appear to be the wing-like reserves.

Page 30 **AVA**

This pattern was made by T.J. & J. Mayer. The plate shown in Book I was a backstamp that reads only "Stone Ware", no maker is indicated. The same size plate with identical pattern has been located marked T.J. & J. Mayer, Prize Medalist 1851". Made by Thomas , John and James Mayer, GMK. 2570, 1843-55.

Page 35 **CASHMERE**

    The pink cup plate photographed bears a narrow ribbon border. The larger plate shown is green and carries the wide ribbon band that covers the cavetto and invades the well. Note that the center designs differ slightly on various sized dishes, but most contain a central bouquet flanked by a pair of exotic birds. There is one bird on the cup plate.

Page 36   **DAVENPORT I**

The dish shown in Book I is printed in pink. Here is the same plate and its backstamp.

Page 38 **EXCELSIOR**

The cup plate shown in Book I is not Excelsior. It is Amula. (See this book, Floral Category, for Amula.)

Page 46 **PAXTON**

The plate shown in Book I is printed in mulberry and over coloured with green and red. This pattern was also made in Flow Blue.

Page 57   **AGRICULTURAL VASE**

In the foreground of the plate photographed the vase of the title is placed at right and the background scene fills the left section of the dish. In the center distance cattle are being led across a long wooden plank bridge. This view was taken from an engraving by W.H. Bartlett. It is a Canadian scene, "Outlet of Lake Memphremagog". This lake rises in Vermont and extends eight miles to the Canadian border in Quebec. The bridge scene has been enlarged so the details can be noted. This same view was used by Francis Morley on his "Lake" pattern.

The toothbrush box shown carries the border spray design on the outside, and the vase at left center on both its cover and on the bottom of the inside. The famous bridge scene is not included.

AGRICULTURAL VASE (cont.)

AGRICULTURAL VASE (cont.)

Page 58   **ANTIQUES**

Hicks, Meigh and Johnson used the term "Stone China". Godden, page 323, c. 1830.

Page 59   **ANTIQUE VASES**

Found marked "J.C." Probably Joseph Clementson. See Godden, page 723, 1841-64.

Page 60 **ARCADIAN CHARIOTS**

The dish (10") photographed is printed in medium blue and white. The picture of the temple is clear and so is that of the charioteer. There are other men on horses at left. The rim design is different from that used on the light blue and white vases shown in Book I, and consists of triangles of white acanthus design separated by dark scroll-like spears. The backstamps are different also, that on the vase consists of the title framed by a vine. (Illus.) The dish is backstamped by Cauldon. G.M.K. 821, 1905+. This could be a re-issue of an original pattern of John Ridgway Bates or Brown-Westhead, Moore and Co. as Cauldon succeeded these firms.

ARCADIAN CHARIOTS (cont.)

Page 61   **ATHENA**

Re the mark "M.T. & Co." Wakefield in his book "Victorian Pottery"
lists Marple, Turner & Co. for 1852.

Page 62   **CLAREMONT**

The grey and white soup plate is backstamped by Joseph Clementson
and is marked as shown J. Clementson, and Ironstone, also (imp.) Cle-
mentson, Shelton, and dated for registration on June 30, 1856.

The pitcher illustrated is printed with a grey transfer and coloured
under the glaze with red, blue, green, yellow and bronze. The border
pattern of twisted rope, floral garland twisting between large loops, and
stylized white acanthus, is placed around the collar. A reduced version was
applied around the base. The vases and flowers differ from those shown on
the plate but the placement is about the same.

Marked C.B. and an embossed Rg. No. 19886 which could indicate a
date around 1885. It is also stamped Royal Semi-Porcelain, a term used
after 1883. The pitcher would seem to be a late re-issue.

CLAREMONT (cont.)

CLAREMONT (cont.)

Page 73 **MYCENE**

The plate shown in Book I (10") is ten sided with a panelled concave rim. It is printed in blue and white. The backstamp (shown here) is marked H. N. & A. The round sepia and white toy saucer (4") has a different backstamp. The border pattern is not as elaborate as the larger dishes and the small vignettes have a different classical figure of a woman with an urn, a lyre and a swan. The toy dishes are also printed in blue and red and probably green and black; all are made in a simple round mold. Marked W.A.A. for William Alsagar Adderly, GMK. 47, 1876-1905. The plate in Book I by Hulse, Nixon & Adderly dates 1853-68. That company was succeeded by Hulse & Adderly (1869-75) so dishes probably can be found with the mark H. & A. (GMK. 2132).

MYCENE (cont.)

Page 80 **"URN AND ROSES"**

The correct name according to Robert Copeland, Esq. is "Antique Vase". It is printed with a soft creamy gold border and a green center transfer.

Page 81 **VERSAILLES**

Was made by Joseph Goodwin. Marked Tunstall and Ironstone China. Mark not listed in Godden.

Page 84 **WASHINGTON VASE**

Has been located in lavender, medium blue, Flow Blue, and most famous of all, in mulberry.

Oriental Category

Page 89   **ALADDIN**

Here we show the same large plate as photographed in Book I in order to show the difference in appearance between the dish and the cup plate in the pattern. The transfer on the little plate omits the boat and most of the exotic buildings at the right.

ALADDIN (cont.)

Page 95 and 96   **ASIATIC VIEWS**

Here is a plate with a different central scene and shown are the Podmore Walker and Dillon backstamps. This printing is in a very pale blue.

Page 98   **BELZONI**

   This pattern was manufactured in many colours: blue, red, green, black, probably sepia, and many combinations of the above. The platter photographed here has a red border and a blue central picture. It presents the same border with the two pairs of reserves that is seen on page 99. The central scene shows a woman in flowing headdress and gown who kneels before a bareheaded man who holds a long spear. Nearby another man with a cap, also holding a spear, stands next to two small horses. There are temple ruins on a promontory at right. Tropical trees rise at left. A river divides the scene and in the background there are two sailboats pulled up to shore and three men nearby.

Page 104   **CANTON VIEWS**

This cup plate is printed in a heavy medium blue. The central scene covers the well, contains no figures on boats and is only identified by the heavy rocks and large tree, and white stones from the foreground featured on the larger plates.

Page 110   **CHINESE FOUNTAINS**

The object photographed in the first book was a platter which is printed in lavender. Here is shown a cup plate in pale blue; it is presented in order to show the way the border pattern looks in the round. The back-stamp was taken from the platter.

Page 112   **CHINESE JUVENILE SPORTS**

Shown here is a platter in order to demonstrate the way the transfer border design appears when it is elongated. The central scene shows children at play with various small toys and seated near them is a toy seller with a cart full of playthings. In the background on a hill there is a large turreted castle.

Page 115 **CHINESE PASTIME**

Here is a small plate that shows children in a fishing scene.

Page 118 **"CHINOISERIE AFTER PILLEMONT"**

A green and white scalloped cup plate is shown. The design covers the entire surface of the little dish and presents a Chinese lady standing on a platform with an attendant who holds a parasol over her head.

This cup plate, or childs dish (4") is printed in green. The little dishes shown in Book I are printed in black.

Page 120   **DAMASCUS**

*The dish photographed is a late copy of the old pattern made by
Adams. The ornate border of the older dishes has been omitted and a single
band of acanthus is placed around the edge. Marked Baker & Co. Ltd.
Made by W. Baker & Co. Like GMK. 232, c. 1893.*

Page 124   **EQUESTRIAN VASE AND ALEXANDRIA**

According to a Scottish correspondent, Equestrian Vase was made by James Couper & Sons of the City Pottery, Glasgow, Scotland 1850-53. Since Godden does not list the mark for Sons with J.C. (Joseph Clementson) this may be correct. She adds that Alexandria turned up frequently in Scotland and is possibly Bo'ness (John Marshall & Co., Bo'ness, Scotland, GMK. 2509, 1854-99).

Page 127   **INDIA TEMPLE**

Here is a cup plate with the same center transfer as shown on the plate and cup plate in the first book, however this little dish has a gadroon edge that matches the larger plate.

Page 130   **JAPAN**

The platter shown in Book I was printed in black. Here is a dinner plate (10½") printed in light grey and over painted with soft pastel colours of rose, green, orange, yellow, sepia, tan and blue. Note the Chinese key design set in six places around the embossed edge. This pattern was also made in Flow Blue. The plate is backstamped J. & M.P.B. & Co. and (imp.) "Royal".

Page 131   **JAPAN FLOWERS**

This pattern is shown in Book I as it appears on a green plate and on a lavender cup plate. The platter photographed is printed in blue, is gently lobed, measures 15" x 19", and contains the entire central scene used in this transfer. The large flat urn is at left filled with the flowers of the title. There is part of a balustrade in the center and a tall vase is at right.

Page 144   **MOGUL SCENERY**

The cup plate shown in Book I is printed in mulberry. The tureen set shown was printed in sepia. Here is a plate (10″) printed in black which displays the garland border. The central picture shows an elephant with howdah, palm trees, a river with a covered boat pulled up to shore and a cenotaph or temple with two minarets in the background.

Page 147   **NANKING**

The plate (8") shown in Book I is printed in sepia. The cup plate is grey and white, and a dinner plate (10") printed in light blue which shows a couple dressed in long Chinese robes who stand on a terrace at right. Tall trees rise in the foreground and there are many buildings with curved roofs in the background.

NANKING (cont.)

Page 158   **PEKIN**

    Here is a platter that shows the entire central scene. There are five figures that include a seated mandarin and a servant holding a parasol over the aristocratic head. The border design of leafy sprigs set over a random wormtrack pattern appears to consist of slanting rows of the leaves.

Page 163   **SINGANESE**

*Singanese has been found marked W.F. & Co. (Whittington Ford &
Co., 1868-73).*

Page 168   **TIPPECANOE**

*The dish photographed is a cup plate (4"). It shows the entire border.
Note that Singanese and Tippecanoe are the same pattern so the cup plate
cannot be attributed definitely.*

Page 169   **VIEWS IN MESOPOTAMIA**

Note that the title in Book I is incorrect. Here is a pierced dish (8") in the pattern. It is completely covered in Bristol blue and the design is printed in black. The plate (10") shown in Book I is light blue and white.

Page 173   **ABBEY**

Here is a better picture of the pale blue plate and the backstamps both printed and impressed.

Page 177   **ACROPOLIS**

This pattern has been found with the mark H.&C. Possibly Hope & Carter, GMK. 2088, 1862-80. Hope was formerly with Pinder Bourne & Hope (1851-62). Pinder was Thomas Pinder of Burslen (1849-51). Acropolis may have been made by any of these companies.

Page 179   **ADELAIDES BOWER**

The plate shown in Book I is mulberry. Here is the same central scene on an eight inch plate which is printed in black. The cup plate is printed in medium blue.

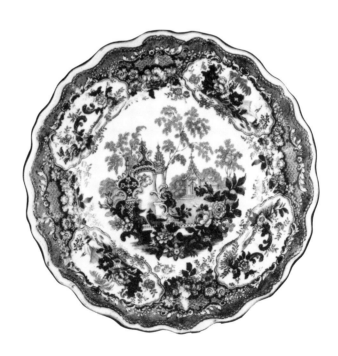

ADELAIDES BOWER (cont.)

Page 184 **ANCIENT RUINS**

    This pattern was presented in Book I and showed a greyish green tureen stand. Many different colours were used in the printings of this pattern. The soup dish photographed shows the border pattern of vertical lacey flower strewn swags at the upper edge and flower garlands at the base of the rim. The central scene has ruins at left and a fountain in the center background. A standing man and a seated woman are placed in the foreground. The plate is printed in light blue.

    The cup plate, which is red and white, omits most of the border with the exception of the distinguishing upper section of vertical lacey drapery. The central scene shows the same couple in the foreground and open arches in the background.

    The small pitcher printed in cobalt shows part of the vertical lacey pattern at the collars edge and part of the garlands. Ruined arches are at left. Two men, one with a spear, stand in the center and there is a tall fountain at right.

ANCIENT RUINS (cont.)

Page 185 **ANDALUSIA**

    The plate shown in Book I is printed in red. Here is a different center scene of a man and lady who are out riding with a greyhound racing in front of them. It is printed in black.

Page 186 **ANTIQUARIAN**

Here is a sugar bowl in the pattern which shows the deer in the foreground in greater detail. The border pattern is the same as that around the outer edge of the plate and consists of little white scrolls that give a dentil effect. The cup plate photographed has the same lacey rim design as the large plate, but the garland and the little basket featured on the border of the larger plate are omitted. On the cup plate a Gothic tower is at right. The antlers of one deer can be seen at lower foreground left; the other deer is omitted.

ANTIQUARIAN (cont.)

Page 190   **ARCHIPELEGO**

The large pink plate is photographed again for this edition in order to show the difference in the pale blue cup plate center picture. There is only one boat shown on the small plate.

Page 191   **ARDENNE**

Here is a cup plate of the pattern. The large monument is at right and the castle buildings are in the left background. There are no human figures in the scene.

Page 194   **BARONIAL HALLS**

    The scene on the pink printed cup plate is dominated by a rider on a rearing horse at left center. The man wears a Robin Hood hat with a feather and carries a lance. The castle entrance flanked by tall towers is in the background. The larger plates are shown in Book I; one is printed in purple (shown here again), the other is in blue. Both contain many human figures and small dogs.

BARONIAL HALLS (cont.)

Page 201   **BOLOGNA**

Here is the same plate that was photographed for Book I. Also shown is a sauce tureen stand with a different scene. The plate is printed in mulberry and the little stand is printed in pink and green. Note that the oblong key shapes of the lower border on the plate were also used in the backstamp.

BOLOGNA (cont.)

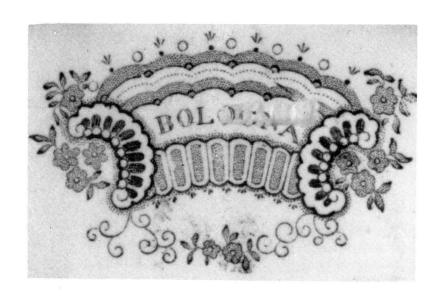

Page 205   **BRITISH LAKES**

British Lakes has been found marked R.S. & S. (Ralph Stevenson & Sons) GMK. 3706, 1832-35. The item photographed in Book I is a toddy plate (4¾") printed in sepia with an incomplete backstamp. Here is a picture of a ten inch dinner plate printed in blue and white and back-stamped as shown R.S. & S. Another plate photographed out of the studio showed a different center scene and was marked H & V. This may have been the mark of a retailer who didn't want a factory mark on his china because customers might go directly to the source. The pink cup plate shown does not carry the distinctive Japanese style border and can be identified only by the rustic Gothic style house in the left middle ground which also appears on the blue dish. The pitcher printed in blue and white has no markings. Although all the other dishes shown have two persons in the foreground, the pitcher carries a scene with cattle standing on the foreground banks.

BRITISH LAKES (cont.)

BRITISH LAKES (cont.)

Page 207   **BRITISH SCENERY**

Coysh lists eight different scenes in the series including the one shown in Book I which he entitled "The Windmill".

Page 208   **BRUSSELS**

Here is a picture of the same blue plate as shown in Book I and its backstamp.

Page 214   **CANOVA**

    The sugar bowl and creamer photographed here bear a different scene from those catalogued before. The scene appears in Book I on page 724 as Unknown Genre number 9 where it was noted that the trees in the picture resemble those in Canova. Here is the sugar bowl on which the scene appears in full transfer; also a cream pitcher which shows the scene of a troubador and the lady on a terrace. The covered dish shown has the same pattern on the side, the top has holes in it to let steam escape. The hollo-ware and cups and saucer all carry this scene. Canova was printed in many colours and many colour combinations.

CANOVA (cont.)

Page 216   **CANOVIAN**

When the famous Italian sculptor Canova died in 1822 his heart was supposedly placed in an urn and put in the wall of a church in Venice. He had visited London in 1815 and the English potters memorialized him with many transfer patterns containing urns. "Washington Vase" by Podmore Walker was one of these. Clews used the urn in the cup plate shown in Book I. Here is another picture of the cup plate which is printed in red. The large plate (10") in Book I is printed in mulberry, the seven inch plate in black. The backstamp is taken from the mulberry plate. The cup plate is marked with an impressed asterisk.

Page 218   **CAROLINA**

  *Here is a different scene and the backstamp on a black printed dish.
The large plate in Book I is printed in purple, the cup plate in a purplish
red.*

Page 220   **CASHIOBERRY**

    Noted at an antique show was a plate in the series entitled Wortham Abbey, backstamp of a little man holding a sign board. This mark was reissued in 1931. See GMK. 4291.

Page 221 **CASSINO**

The item shown is a muffineer. It is not marked but note the border edging around the plate is the same as the collar on the muffineer. It is printed in light purple. The large plate shown in Book I is printed in green, the cup plate in blue.

Page 222   **CASTLE SCENERY**

Here is a picture of the dish (10″) shown in Book I, and a photograph of a sugar bowl showing the border used around the collar. The sugar bowl is unmarked. The backstamp is taken from the dish.

CASTLE SCENERY (cont.)

Page 225 **CHANTILLY I**

The lavender dish (10″) photographed in Book I is shown here in order to demonstrate that the cup plate printed in blue is not scalloped and the upper part of the border design has been omitted.

Page 227   **CHATEAU**

The bottom section of the blue and white butter dish is photographed. Notice the strong concentric lines, white scrolls and floral reserves in the border design. The cup plate, also blue and white, bears the same center scene but no human figures are pictured.

Page 235   **COLOGNE**

   *Here is a black, grey and white vegetable dish in this pattern. Note the
way the border design was affixed to conform to the square dish. The
central scenes differ on the various items made in the pattern. The two cup
plates shown in Book I are respectively mulberry and purple. The other
dishes are green and blue.*

Page 242 **CORINTH (Edwards)**

Here is an eight inch dish in the pattern. It is printed in sepia. It bears the same transfer as the ten inch plate shown in Book I which is printed in light blue. The cup plate is also sepia (enlarged photo) and contains only one figure in the foreground.

CORINTH (Edwards) (cont.)

Page 243   **CORINTH (Phillips)**

Here is a picture of a cup plate in the pattern. It is one of a pair; one is red and one is blue. Note the swags composed by the linear border. This is the distinguishing feature of this pattern.

Page 244   **CORINTHIA**

Here is a plate (10") in the pattern but it is marked E. Challinor (Edward Challinor, GMK. 1835A, 1842-67). One of a pair; one is purple and one is red. The Wedgwood & Co. plate (10") is sepia; the little toy dish is black and white.

Page 247   **CRYSTAL PALACE**

A small vegetable dish is photographed. The scene is the same as shown on the cup plate in Book I. The border is the same as shown on the platter. A Scottish correspondent relates that it was not the pattern made by J. & M.P. Bell as the border is different.

See this book for the correct pattern manufactured by J.&M. P. Bell & Co.

Page 251   **DELPHI**

    Here is a dish (10″) printed in blue. Note the border design when used in the round. The platter in Book I is also printed in blue.

Page 253   **DORIA**

   Photographed is a cup plate in the pattern. The Tuscan mansion in the center of the scene is different from that on the dish (10″) shown in Book I. There are no people or boats, nor is there a balustrade or tree at right on the small dish.

Page 254 **EASTERN SCENERY**

Here is a 10″ plate. It is printed in medium blue as is the platter shown in Book I.

Page 255   **ENGLISH CITIES**

   A plate with a different city scene is photographed and also shown is a cup plate which has no central circle of spearpoint around the center scene which covers the well. Note that the border pattern has been truncated. The plate is printed in black; the cup plate is blue and white. The plates shown in Book I are printed in sepia.

Page 257   **EON**

    Shown here is a plate (9″) with a different scene printed in blue. The windmill is in the left background and shepherds and sheep are under a tree in the foreground. The plate in Book I has a mulberry border and a blue center scene.

Page 260 **EUROPEAN SCENERY**

Here are two more scenes from the series. The plates in the first book are printed in black. The dish (10″) that shows a mosque is printed in sepia; the other (9″) is printed in red.

Page 263   **FLORENTINE VILLAS**

Here is a clearer picture of the blue plate (10″) shown in Book I and two cup plates in the pattern.

FLORENTINE VILLAS (cont.)

Page 265 **FOUNTAIN SCENERY**

Here are two different scenes, one plate (8″) with a goat on the pedestal near the tall fountain at left, and the other (10″) with a horse statue. The ten inch plate is printed with a black border and purple center. The eight inch plate is reversed with a purple border and a black center. The two dishes shown in Book I are printed in red.

Page 267   **FRIBURG**

Here is a blown up photograph of the cup plate found in this pattern. It is printed in blue as is the plate shown in Book I. The pattern has been found marked G. Phillips Longport (George Phillips, Exact GMK. 3012, 1834-84).

Page 268   **GARDEN SCENERY**

Here is a different center scene enlarged to show detail. These dishes are printed in pale blue.

Page 269 **GEM**

Illustrated is a plate in the pattern. It is marked S.B. & S. It was made by Samuel Barker & Son, GMK. 267, 1851-93. Both the dish and the platter shown in Book I are printed in blue.

Page 272 **GENEVA**

The item photographed is a cup plate. The center scene is different from that shown in Book I on a large dish (10"). Both are printed in light blue. On the cup plate the flight of stone steps is at center. The newel topped with a stone urn is at right, and there is a similar urn at the top of the stairs. There are several small white figures over the railing and on the steps. They may be white flowers or a flock of small white birds.

Page 274   **GENEVESE**

Here is a pitcher by Minton in the pattern that is printed with a variation of the scene and contains human figures in the foreground. A dish marked Genevese, marked T. & B. Godwin, New Wharf (imp.) has been found with the same border as that of Minton which is shown on the plate at the top left of page 275, but the center scene is the same as Swiss Scenery in Book I on page 428. Marked Opaque China and (imp.) Minton.

Page 284   **GRECIAN GARDENS**

The cup plate illustrated has almost the same design as the larger dish shown in Book I, except that the statue of the goddess at left is different and the background details are arranged somewhat differently. Both plates are printed in pink. Shown are two backstamps, The Wreath appears on the plate shown in Book I.

Page 288   **GRECIAN SCENERY**

The plate photographed contains a different center scene than that shown in Book I. This scene is dominated by a large urn at left from which a tall fountain rises. There are temples in the right background. A man holding a pole stands facing a girl who wears a peaked hat like those found on ancient Tanagra figurines. She is seated on a rock in the right foreground. Both the plate and the one shown in Book I are printed in a soft greyish blue.

Page 295 **HUDSON**

The cup plate illustrated is enlarged to show the details. The border pattern is especially clear. The central scene is the same as that on the larger plate but contains no human figures. It is printed in pale blue.

Page 296 **ILLUSTRATIONS OF THE BIBLE**

Here is another plate (9½″) in the pattern. It is entitled "Fountain of Elisha at Jericho". The center scene shows a large pool with stone coping. A crane stands in the water at left. Three men, one of whom is seated on a rock, converse on a bank in the right foreground. Tall trees are placed across the background. A single large white bird flies over the pool at middle right. The dish is printed in purple as is the large plate (10″) shown in Book I. The shallow bowl shown in Book I is printed in green.

Page 297   **INDIAN TEMPLE**

This pattern is miscatalogued. See this book for listing in Oriental Category.

Page 299   **ISOLA BELLA**

Here is a better picture of the cup plate.

Page 300   **ITALIA**

Italia has been found marked T. Fell & Co. The bowl photographed carries the scenic transfer on the outside and the border pattern on the inside at top. Marked T.F. & Co., Thomas Fell & Co., GMK. 1534, c. 1830-90.

Page 307   **ITALY**

The toy plate shown in Book I displays only the center scene. Here is a saucer that displays the border design of grapes alternating with ovals composed of foliated scrolls set over a background of narrow concentric lines. The outer edge is covered with a band of triangles and the well is surrounded by a wreath of darts and beaded ovals. The center scene is the same as that shown on the toy dish. Both are printed in a pinkish red. The mark should read GMK. 1441, c. 1873.

Page 310   **JENNY LIND**

     This pattern is usually found printed in grey and over coloured on small details with red and green. The item photographed is a cup plate which is printed in purple.

Page 316   **LOMBARDY**

The cup plate illustrated is almost a duplicate of the larger plate shown in Book I with the exception that there is only one gondola in the foreground. It is printed in light blue.

Page 319   **LOZERE**

Illustrated is the 10″ dinner plate in the pattern. It is printed in light blue as are the dishes shown in Book I. Lozere was also made in Flow Blue.

Page 320 **LUCERNE**

Here is a plate and a cup plate. The plate (10″) displays the same scene as that on the bowl shown in Book I. The cup plate transfer presents a bit of Swiss scenery, a lake, bridge, small chalet, and pine trees and elms at right. The plate and cup plate are marked (imp.) J. Clementson, Stoneware and Shelton. The plate is also marked (ptd.) J.C. and "Granite Ware". GMK. 910A.

Page 321   **LUCERNE**

*The makers name is mispelled. It is Pankhurst & Co. (not Parkhurst).
Shown here is the same plate and its backstamp.*

Page 324 **MANSION**

This plate is marked (imp.) Edwards Ironstone. It was probably made by James and Thomas Edwards (like G.M.K. 1456, 1839-41). It bears the same center scene as the soup dish shown in Book I. Also illustrated is the center scene found on the large platter. The small two handled urn on the platform at right center is also pictured on the cup plate shown in Book I. All the dishes are printed in blue.

599

MANSION (cont.)

Page 327   **MARINO**

    Examples of this pattern have been found with a later pottery date of Thomas Till & Son, GMK. 3854, 1850-61.

    This cup plate, printed in pink bears the backstamp of George Phillips. Most dishes found in the pattern are printed in light blue.

Page 330 **MARYLAND**

A correspondent from England, who has just completed a study about Samuel Alcock, confirms that the mark of the beehive and Florentine China was indeed the mark of Samuel Alcock. The plate illustrated in Book I is printed in purple and so is the backstamp which is shown here.

Page 333   **MEDICI**

    This photograph pictures the outside border pattern on a bowl. Note that the urn set in its scrolled reserve differs from those used on the borders of flat dishes. The urn is short and wide, those on dishes are tall and narrow. The bowl is not marked with a pattern name. Both bowl and 9" plate are printed in pale blue.

MEDICI (cont.)

Page 334   **MESINA**

    This little dish (3¾″) shown, which is deep enough to hold honey, has the same scene as the larger dish illustrated in Book I except that there are no people pictured. The cup plate is printed in blue, the larger plate in mulberry.

MESINA (cont.)

Page 337   **MILANESE PAVILIONS**

The plate shown bears a different scene from that shown in Book I and so does the platter. The plate is printed in mulberry, the platter in rose. The dish (8″) shown in Book I is printed in purple.

Page 340   **MISSOURI**

The cup plate shown was made at a later date. It does not have the typical Missouri wormtrack border but does contain the same central scene. Marked E.M. & Co. Made by Edge, Malkin & Co., GMK. 1441, 1871-1903.

Page 342   **MONOPTERIS**

Photographed here is a toy plate shown in Book I and a large platter (20" plus). They contain the same scene. Note the elongation of the transfer design and of the scene and border when used on the platter. Both are printed in a strong medium blue.

Page 350   **NON PAREIL**

Upon closer observation both plates shown in Book I are marked T. & J. Mayer Longport. This mark is not recorded in Godden. Thomas Mayer potted from 1836-38. We read that Thomas Mayer, John and Joseph worked 1843-55. The mark on these dishes is clearly T. & J. Mayer (Illus.). Perhaps Thomas worked with John from 1838-43 when they were joined by Joseph.

Here are two cup plates. Each has the same center scene but the borders are different and one has fern fronds near the stylized flowers. The impressed small marks on the backs differ also. The one on the less ornate border is a quarter circle; the other an asterisk. It could be concluded that the different borders and backstamps are from different periods of the Mayer's work.

The platter (20″) photographed is printed in blue. It contains an exotic scene of temples, minarets and tropical trees. An ornate carriage drawn by a pair of oxen is near the center of the scene. Men dressed in turbans and long shirts stand near the cart. Other men are grouped by the small temple at right. A river divides the scene and there are mountain peaks in the distance. One of the plates shown in Book I is printed in sepia; the other in green. The cup plates are light blue and brown respectively. The platter is printed in a strong blue.

NON PAREIL (cont.)

NON PAREIL (cont.)

Page 351   **OBERWESSEL**

    For a fuller description of the border design, refer to Cetero (Bay of Salerno), and Venice, this book.

Page 353   **ONTARIO LAKE SCENERY**

    This pattern has been found marked with the same backstamp but B. & D. instead of Heath. Also found with impressed propeller mark in a beaded circle.

Page 356   **PALESTINE**

   The cup plate photographed is printed in blue as is the wash basin shown in Book I. (Illustrated.) The cup plate presents in miniature a replica of the central scene on the basin.

Page 357   **PALMYRA**

Found marked T. Furnival & Co. Registered date for 1845 (Thomas Furnival & Co., see Godden page 263).

Page 361   **PANTHEON**

The bowl illustrated in Book I does not provide a clear picture of the sprig filled wormtrack design of the border. Here are pictures of a plate and soup dish with different center scenes which illustrate the border. Note the scalloped and fleur-de-lis wreath which contains it at the well. The bottom of the covered dish shown in Book I is printed in green and the scene in the center has been over coloured in many colours. The plate (9") is printed in a pinkish red and the soup dish in light blue.

PANTHEON (cont.)

Page 362   **PARISIAN**

Here are pictures of a plate (10″) and a cup plate in the pattern. The border design of mossy sprigs is inset with stylized six petalled rosettes with dark centers that alternate with a trio of floweretts. There are no human figures in the scene on the cup plate.

Page 366   **PARMA**

Has been identified by a correspondent from England as marked E.C. (Edward Challinor, GMK. 855, 1842-67). She also states that the identical pattern, also printed in blue and white, has the backstamp with title "Belevedere" and a mark exactly like Ridgway's (John Ridgway & Co., GMK. 3257, 1841-55). See this book.

Page 367 **PEARL**

Here is a different scene and backstamp. It has been confirmed that the mark is that of Samuel Alcock.

Page 375   **PICTURESQUE VIEWS**

     The main title of these three dishes is Hudson River. One shows Baker's Falls; on one the title is Nr Fishkill; the platter shows the city of of Hudson. Note that each center scene is framed by a narrow band of scallops and darts. All are printed in black. These are American views and included in this book because of the interest of the detailed transfer. The platter in Book I is printed in dark blue and is an English view.

PICTURESQUE VIEWS (cont.)

PICTURESQUE VIEWS (cont.)

Page 385   **RAVENNA**

A collector reports finding the pattern marked W. B. Could be William Brownfield, GMK. 660. He used this mark from 1850-71.

Page 386   **RHINE**

Found marked Booth & Meigh, Lane End. Mark not located. Booth & Sons of Church Street, Lane End (GMK. 446) worked from 1830-5. Godden states that they were also listed as Richard and Able Booth.

Page 389   **RHINE RIVER SCENE**

Has been identified as the cup plate in a dinner set entitled "Swiss Village and Lake". See this book.

Page 390   **RHONE SCENERY**

Here is the cup plate in the pattern. Note that the border is the same as on the larger plate but vertical bars are placed between the garlands. Perhaps as in the case of Non Pariel by the Mayers, the borders were changed during the potting period.

Page 391   **"ROMANTIC"**

The correct name is Manilla. Samuel Alcock & Co. has been identi-fied as the potter.

Page 394   **ROUSILLON**

The picture of the cup plate illustrated has been enlarged to show border detail. The center scene is the same as that on the larger plate shown in Book I with the exception that there is only one human figure in the foreground. Both dishes are printed in pale blue.

Page 397   **"RUINS"**

Here is the pattern as used on the round dishes. Note the man with the pole and two cows in the foreground. Three youth are playing on the platform and steps of the ruined temple. Little shows this pattern on plate 4 and says the scene was designed by William Brook of Portvale, Walstamton, after a picture by Claude Lorrain.

Page 408   **SCOTTISH MINSTREL**

Here is a better picture of the central scene which shows the minstrel of the title standing in the foreground as a lady holds his arm.

Page 411 **SEINE**

The maker's name should read John Wedge Wood.

Page 412 **SELECT VIEWS**

It is illustrated to show the border detail. Note the resemblance to Spanish Convent. The plate shown in Book I is printed in black.

Page 414 **SEVILLA**

This pattern has been found marked Spanish Beauty made by Deakin. See this book for details.

Page 416   **SICILIAN**

   The cup plate shown at the top right is incorrectly ascribed to Sicilian. It is Adelaides Bower. Illustrated is a platter in the pattern and an enlarged photograph of the correct cup plate.

SICILIAN (cont.)

Page 418 **"SICILY"**

This cup plate is from the Byron View Series. It pictures Mt. Etna.

Page 420 **SPANISH CONVENT**

The title is misspelled. The correct title is Spanish Convent. Here is a cup plate in the pattern that was shown in Book I as Unknown Scenic US 22. A comparison of the borders proves the relationship. The dishes are usually printed in red, sometimes in black, the cup plate in red with green border or vice-versa. Note that Select Views has the same border but the central scenes of Spanish Convent are always framed by a wreath of sprigs. This is not true of Select Views.

SPANISH CONVENT (cont.)

Page 427   **"SWISS"**

A plate with oriental figures has been catalogued. It is marked 107 and listed in this book in the Oriental Category as "Canton 107". The plate in Book I is printed in blue; the "Canton 107" is in sepia and is over coloured.

Page 428   **SWISS SCENERY**

Swiss Scenery has been found marked (imp.) Stubbs. GMK. 3728, c. 1822-35.

Page 437   **TYROLEON**

The large plate (10") shown is printed in green and it has a different scene from those shown on the dishes shown in Book I. The smaller dish is a cup plate and it is printed in green and it, too, has a different scene. It shows a single standing shepherd who holds a hook and white sheep on either side of him. The pine trees and tall elm are at right, smaller pines, castle and a town at left. The plate (8") in Book I is printed in purple and the cup plate in light blue.

TYROLEON (cont.)

Page 439 **UNION**

This cup plate is printed in blue. It shows the farmer standing beside his plow and a team of horses. The other human figures shown on the larger mulberry plate (see Book I) are omitted.

Page 448   **VENETIAN TEMPLE**

Here is a cup plate that is completely different from the one shown in Book I. A photograph of the larger plate from Book I is shown here again in order to compare the border and the center scene on this cup plate. The boat, which is a distinguishing feature of the pattern, is used in the border of this cup plate. The man standing next to the temple is also placed in the border next to the temple columns. All the dishes in the design are printed in pink. The picture in the bottom of the handless cup is the same shown in the center of the cup plate. (not illustrated).

Page 452   **VENUS**

    A cup plate is illustrated; the transfer carries only one white swan in the foreground. This is different from the other dishes in the pattern which always contain two swans.

Page 456   **VILLA**

The saucer photographed has a different scene from that shown on the plate in Book I. The villa of the title is at left and there is no bridge in the picture. A woman leans over a basket set on the lawn at left center. Another woman stands near her and a man is seated on the base of a pedestal at left. The view on the side of the large vegetable dish is about the same as that shown on the tureen in Book I. These dishes are printed in greyish soft green and sepia with gold trim.

VILLA (cont.)

Page 461 **VIRGINIA**

Here is a plate printed in black that illustrates in sharp detail this transfer design. Note the distinguishing curving double horns at the top of the border pattern.

Page 463   **VISTA**

Here is a cup plate in this pattern. Also shown is a toy platter (5"), which is printed in light black and grey on white. The plate shown in Book I and the toy plate are both blue and white.

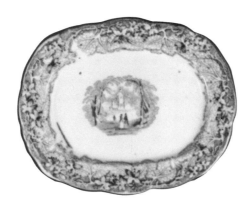

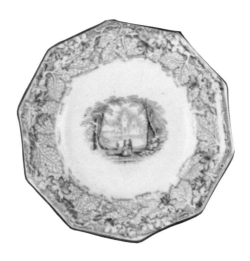

Page 471   **ARCHERY**

The central scene on this salad plate is the same as shown on the cup plate in Book I. The wreath on this dish is the same as that on the larger plate but the cavetto and the space between the wreath and the border design is molded into deep oval depressions. This plate is blue and white. The cup plate in Book I is printed in blue, the dinner plate (10″) in sepia.

Page 480   **COLUMBUS**

   The larger plate shown in Book I and again here for comparison is 10″ in diameter and is pink. The smaller plate shown in Book I, 5″ in diameter, is green. Here is a 4″ plate, the cup plate in the series, also green. It has exactly the same border, of course. The central scene is different and shows some ships in the foreground and the tall mountain peaks in the background. The backstamp which we show here is taken from the large 10″ plate.

Page 484   **CRUSADERS**

Made by Deakin & Bailey

    This pattern is shown in Book I. That bowl, which is mulberry, does not have a backstamp. Here is a plate in the pattern which shows the border design with the lacy lambrequins and roses and a different central scene of a man on a white horse approaching a gate near which a young girl stands. The plate photographed in this book is brown.

    Marked as above. Dated by Little, c. 1828-30. Mark not located.

Page 485 **DANCERS**

A wrong mark was given in the first book. The exact GMK. is 2493.

ETON COLLEGE

This pattern was recently seen by the author on an ornate flow blue boat-shaped flower container.
Unmarked.

Page 497 **HARVEST HOME**

Made by James & Ralph Clews

The platter is from the Dr. Syntax series. The man playing the fiddle is Dr. Syntax. This dish is from the series illustrating the Third Tour, "Dr. Syntax's Tour in Search of a Wife (#25)."

According to research by Coysh, these were made for the American market, the patterns based on drawings by T. Rowlandson, published first in a magazine and then book form. The "Harvest Home" appears in the third volume in 1821. The drawings were illustrations for verses composed by W. Coombe who was in prison for debt for 43 years. The verse appears in "Old China" magazine. Vol. III, July 1904.

In front the mingled groups appear
Of jovial peasants who employ
Their voices loud, in hymns of joy.
Then came the lab'ring waggon's load
Dragg'd on along the winding road,
Rich with the sheaves the harvest yields,
The closing bounty of the fields...
Syntax would now his skill display
Among the minstrels of the day,
And ask'd a fiddle to be sought;
The instrument was quickly brought;
It answered to his active hand,
When he march'd on and led the band.

Page 499 **HAWKING**

According to a Scottish correspondent the mark is R.H.F.P. Robert Heron Fye Pottery in Scotland, c. 1850.

Page 501   **HUMPHREYS CLOCK**

A toy plate like that shown on page 502 has been identified by a correspondent as marked John Ford & Co., Edinborough. John Ford & Co. were retailers, c. 1891-26.

Page 509   **NAPOLEON**

Four items are pictured on page 510. Here is a third cup plate. The border is the famous Napoleon border design of trophies and flowers, and in the center scene a lone figure stands on a bank of a river or the sea. He is wearing a dark jacket and pants, and is looking across at an island which is surmounted by a fortress. This pattern has been noted in pale blue, light purple, black and green.

Page 511   **OLYMPIC GAMES**

Note the border description in Book I which describes the stippled rim. Between the reserves there is a distinctive design composed of a fan and top set upon a scrolled stem which is flanked by pairs of flowers. This may be meant to represent the Olympic torch. Here is a different scene and it is backstamped "Running". Also we show the backstamp of the pattern "Spanish Bull Fight" which is shown in Book I.

Page 519   **SCOTT'S ILLUSTRATIONS (WAVERLY)**

This pattern is shown in Book I on pages 519 and 520. Here is a different center scene. A lady in a white gown with a tartan shawl across her lap holds a harp and is evidently in recital. A gentleman stands behind her. There is a castle and a hill in the background at right.

Marked (imp.) Davenport. GMK. 1179, 1820-60. (Coysh shows this pattern with a dated anchor for 1836).

Page 521 **SEA (THE)**

This little dish is the cup plate of the series. All dishes in the series are printed in pink.

Page 523   **SEASONS**

   Here is a different scene. It is entitled February. A man shovels snow in the foreground. This pattern was made in sepia, pink, black and blue.

Page 525   **SHELTERED PEASANTS**

The cup plate shown has the same central scene as that used on the other dishes in the pattern. The border of flowers and fruits is also the same, however the ring around the central scene is a plain white band as compared to the heavy wreath of white oval beads on the larger dishes.

Page 527   **SPORTING SUBJECTS**

Here is the interesting backstamp used for this pattern.

Page 528   **TEXIAN CAMPAIGN**

This pattern was printed in many colours. The plate and cup plate shown in Book I are in light blue. It has also been found in mulberry.

Page 531 **WILLIAM PENN'S TREATY**

Here is a cup plate in the design. The rim pattern of large zig-zag white crosses and various narrow slanted fringed lines has been eliminated on this little dish. In the center William Penn stands under a willow tree and talks to a seated Indian chief. In the background one sees a river and some town buildings. The pattern was printed in many colours.

Page 533 **ZOOLOGICAL GARDENS**

This small (5¾") plate shows the swan enclosure at the zoo. It is printed in pink. The plate shown in Book I is sepia, its mate has been catalogued in mulberry.

Page 537   **BIRD AT FOUNTAIN**

The plate and pitcher shown are green. The pattern is also found in pale blue.

Juvenile Category

Page 538   **BOY WITH PUNCHINELLO**

A correspondent has this dish with the addition to the title "1851 Exhibition". The drawing for the transfer was made from a statue entitled "The Happy Child" by M. Simonis of Brussels. Perhaps these plates were made to be souvenirs of the Exhibition.

Page 546   **CLOCK**

A better picture of this educational dish.

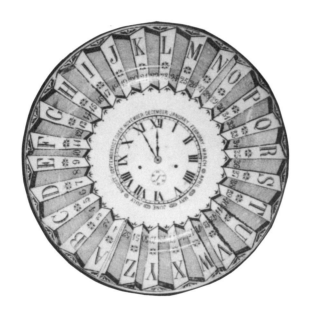

Page 541   **DEAF AND DUMB BUNNY PLATE**
   A clearer picture of this educational dish.

Page 543   **FRANKLIN AND THE KITE**
   According to Coysh in his Encyclopedia, page 204, this pattern should be named "Kite Flying". The transfer was made from a wood engraving by Thomas Berwick in his "History of English Birds" 1797 and 1894. This pattern is found only on toy dishes.

Page 547   **JOSEPHINE AND L'AIGLON**

The former wife of Napoleon is pictured with a child, perhaps the son of Napoleon by his second wife Marie Louise. Josephine remained true to Napoleon after their divorce on the grounds that she was barren. She begged to see the boy and Napoleon did take the child just once to Malmaison, the house he had established for her. The title is conjectural. The transfer may have been made from a drawing by Adam Buck in the early nineteenth century. He portrayed women and children dressed in Grecian style. But the little boy in the scene is dressed in blouse, trousers and a wide sash.

Page 548   **JUVENILE**

This pattern was also made in Flow Blue.

Page 552   **MONASTERY HILL**

Here is a round miniature dish in the pattern.

Page 565   **TEA TIME**

The toy plate shown is from a tea service. A miniature cup and saucer have been located. This pattern was made at the Southerland Potteries in Scotland.

Page 586   **SLAMAT**

Here is a card basket made with the dish as a base. It has a hand twisted wire border and handle. It was termed an "egg basket" by the seller.

Page 593   **VASE WITH PEONY**

According to Robert Copeland this dish has a "Denmark" border and "Canton" center.

Page 609   **BEEHIVE**

Here is the saucer shown in Book I. It is printed in red. Also shown with it is a miniature toy cup and saucer printed in sepia. Some of the details are missing in the transfer on the smaller piece. The toy cup is 2½" and the saucer diameter is 4".

Page 613   **CALEDONIA<u>N</u>**

This was misspelled. The letter N at the end of the word was omitted.

Page 618   **CONCHOLOGY**

Here is a better picture of the dish and its backstamp. The border is printed in pale green, the shells in the center are a soft blue.

Page 619   **CORAL BORDER**

    Photographed is the cup plate of the pattern. Note that the border is omitted from that shown on the transfer of the larger plate. The central bouquet is also different. The cup plate is printed in green; the larger plate (10″) in Book I is blue and white.

Page 625   **FEATHER**

The saucer photographed carries the pattern in a much bolder fashion than that shown on the plate in Book I.

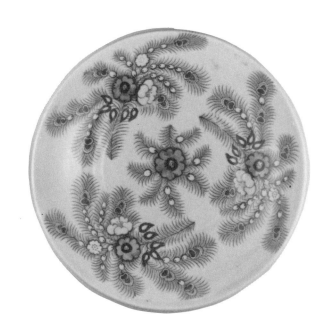

Page 630   **FOREST**

    Forest has been found marked J. Clementson. GMK. 610A, 1839-64. This saucer is printed in sepia.

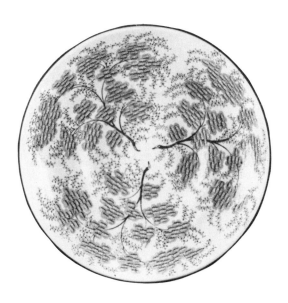

Page 631   **FRUIT AND FLOWERS**

Here is a plate and its backstamp. It is marked H. M .J. (Hicks, Meigh and Johnson), GMK. 2021, 1822-35. The lid and inside bottom of a toothbrush box are also shown. There is no border edging on the box but it is backstamped like the plate. It is printed in dark grey; the plate is blue and white.

FRUIT AND FLOWERS (cont.)

Page 632 **FRUIT BASKET**

A cup plate printed in sepia and a dish (7") in pale green are shown. The plate (10") in Book I is printed in pale blue. Only minor details of the center scene are changed on these dishes.

Page 633   **GIRAFFE**

The platter photographed is printed in blue. The fruit dish in sepia. The scenes are about the same as that shown in Book I except that the tents are placed in the right middle ground.

Page 638   **JAPANESE**

The dish (7⅜″) photographed is red and white. The plate (9″) shown in Book I is printed in black. The details of the center picture differ.

Page 645   **MILLENIUM**

On the cup plate shown most of the central scene has been eliminated and only the child, a cow and the lion are pictured under the word "Peace". It is printed in green. The dish (10") shown in Book I is printed in red. The little plate (6") also photographed is printed in lavender and shows the child, the calf and the lamb. A dish (9") in the collection is printed in sepia and shows all the details as they appear on the ten inch red dish. The Bible pictured above the center scene directly under the "Eye of God" is open to Isaiah Chapter 2, VI, and refers to "The wolf shall also dwell with the lamb, and the leopard shall lie down with the kid, and the calf and the young lion and the fatling together; and a little child shall lead them."

MILLENIUM (cont.)

Page 647   **MOSAIC TRACERY**

Here is a dish (9″) in the pattern and its backstamp. It is printed in cobalt.

Page 657   **POLISH STAR**

The cup plate illustrated is printed in red. The dish (8″) shown in Book I is black and white. It is shown again here so that the differences can be noted. The star of the title covers the center of the small dish. On the larger dish the star is set in a large white area and is surrounded by a wreath of fleur-de-lis in the cavetto.

Page 667   **SEA LEAF**

Here is the cup plate in the pattern. It is backstamped Alcock (imp.). Probably made by Samuel Alcock, 1830-59.

Page 670   **"SPODES ORIENTAL BOUQUET"**

According to Robert Copeland the correct name is "Bang-Up". The pattern was created in 1804. It was taken from Japanese Imari. The outline was printed and the colours of red, blue and gold were filled in by hand.

Page 676   **VINTAGE**

   Here is the cup plate in the pattern. Both the pickle dish shown in Book I and this cup plate are printed in lavender.

Unascribed Patterns

Page 683 **U.F. 1.** *The pattern is either "Chinese Flowers" or "Windsor Flowers" and was made by William Adams & Son, according to Plate LI in "William Adams, An Old English Potter."*

Page 685 **U.F. 6.** *The third sentence should read, "Large dark patterned vase at right." (**Not** at left).*

Page 686 **U.O. 2.** *This is India Pattern, see Book I page 126.*

Page 688 **U.O. 4.** *Coysh named this pattern "Palladian Porch". Maker unknown.*

Page 691 **U.O. 6.** *The dishes in this pattern were usually printed in pink. However, the plate (10") photographed has a dark green center and pink border. They were made by William Adams & Sons, found marked (imp.) Adams. GMK. 18, 1800-64.*

Page 691 **U.O. 7.** *The willow cup plate shown has the identical scene with curved roofs and white veined trees as that shown in Little's "Staffordshire Blue", plate 48. Made by William Radcliffe. Marked R in a star. (See mark 42 in Little.)*

Page 693 **U.O. 10.** *A reader sent a picture of a platter (13 x 17) printed in sepia with this pattern. Here are the details. The cup plate shown in Book I is printed in a bluish mulberry.*

Page 702 **U.S. 6.** *Has been found marked (imp.) Wood. GMK. 4247, 1784+. It is printed in green and red. The second sentence should read "European river scene with a large dark tower dominant and a tall Gothic spire behind it. Saucer contains etc...."*

Page 704 **U.S. 9.** *Found marked Eastern Scenery, E.W. & S. and Wood and Son. GMK. 4260, 1818-46. For details see this book.*

Page 705 **U.S.11.** *Here are two cup plates in the pattern. They are printed in cobalt as are all the other dishes shown in this pattern. Printed here again for comparison is the Tureen Stand.*

PAGE 705 U.S. II (cont.)

Page 707 **U.S. 13.** *Coysh states that the name of this pattern is "British Scenery" marked in a ribbon cartouche.*

Page 707 **U.S. 14.** *Coysh states that this is known as "The Cowman".*

Page 708 **U.S. 15.** *Here is a dish with a different center scene. It is printed in pink. The plate shown in Book I is purple and white.*

Page 709 **U.S. 16.** *Found marked (imp.) H. May be Hackwood. Here is a cup plate in the pattern. The center is printed in cobalt, the border with rose lustre. The correct title has not been found. Some collectors call it "Falls of Killarney" and some "Ross Castle". There is no proof as yet of either.*

Page 710 **U.S. 17.** *The pattern is "Washington". It is marked Clementson & Young. GMK. 911, 1845-71. See this book for description.*

Page 711 **U.S. 18.** *Another saucer, printed in blue border and sepia center has been located. It is marked (imp.) Wood. Probably Enoch Wood & Sons, 1818-46. The saucer photographed in Book I, with the same center scene, is printed with a red border and a green scene.*

Page 712 **U.S. 20.** *Found marked Meigh, also found marked (imp.) T. Mayer Stoke. Named "Gothic" when released by another pottery in Sunderland. For description see Gothic this book.*

Page 712 **U.S. 21.** *Found marked VanDyke, S.A. & Co. Samuel Alcock & Co. For description see this book.*

Page 713 **U.S. 22.** *Found marked Adams. The pattern is Spanish Convent. See addenda description of Spanish Convent in this book.*

Page 713 **U.S. 23.** *A correspondent has a dish in this pattern marked "Fairchild". Mark not listed in Godden. May have been a retailer's mark.*

Page 714 **U.S. 25.** *Here is a better picture of the cup plate.*

Page 715 **U.S. 26.** *Illustrated are another cup plate and a larger dish (8″). Both are printed with multi-coloured landscapes that include a castle ruin. The larger plate shows a thatched cottage at the foot of a hill surmounted by the ruin. The butterfly border is printed in grey on the cup plate and sepia on the other dish.*

682

Page 716 **U.S. 28.** *The pattern is Gothic Beauties. Made by Thomas Ingleby & Co. c. 1834. See this book for description.*

Page 716 **U.S. 29.** *Here is a picture of a dish (10″) that shows the entire border. It is printed in blue. The center scene is the same as that shown on the cup plate in Book I. Another plate (10″) is printed in purple.*

Page 718 **U.S. 31.** *The last sentence should read "This may be Seine."*

Page 719 **U.G. 2.** *Found marked Falconry, J.J. & Co. According to Coysh this is James Jamieson & Co. Bo'ness Pottery Scotland. 1836-54.*

Page 720 **U.G. 3.** *Name is Lasso. Marked such with W. Bourne, Longton. Mark not located but a William Bourne of Longton is listed in Little. Here is a cup plate in the pattern. Note that the border was omitted.*

Page 721 **U.G. 4.** *Lasso. Made by P. Regout & Co. Maastricht, Holland.*

Page 723 **U.G. 7.** *No pattern with the name has been located by the time of publication. It is probably Hannibal in the Alps. For a similar scene see Hannibal Passing the Alps in this book.*

Page 723 **U.G. 8.** *Here is a better picture of the cup plate that is marked (imp.) Adams. GMK. 18, 1800-64.*

Page 724 **U.G. 9.** *This pattern is Canova. See description in the Scenic Addenda this book.*

Page 725 **U.G. 11.** *Pattern is Hannibal Passing the Alps. Made by Knight & Elkin. For description see this book.*

Page 726 **U.G. 14.** *Found marked Ridgway (imp.) in block letters. GMK. 3267 probably John & William Ridgway, 1814-30. Titled "The Blind Boy" according to Coysh.*

Page 727 **U.M. 2.** *Birds and Fruit. Here is a plate (10″) and the backstamp. It is marked L & B which is Londes and Beech, according to Coysh. Mark not located.*

Page 728 **U.M. 3.** *Found with a Ridgway mark. The correct title is Albion. See this book for details.*

Page 728 **U.M. 4.** *A collector has a saucer marked (imp.) Wood. This ware is very light. Could be Enoch Wood, GMK. 4247, 1784+.*

Page 729 **U.M. 5.** *Here is a better picture of the cup plate. It is printed in blue.*

Page 733 **U.M. 14.** *Pattern is Spanish Lady. For description see this book.*

Page 735 **U.M. 19.** *The dish is marked under the scene, "Their Mother's Grave".*

Page 758 *"Classic Bouquet". According to Robert Copeland this pattern is Portland Vase.*

Page 763 *Woodman. Here is a picture of a dish 10″ and a bowl in the pattern. Note the men playing hockey in the right background.*

CORRECTIONS TO GLOSSARY

Page 748 *Arabesque should read: A sinuous undulating or serpentine line; decoration and flowing lines of branches, leaves and scrolls.*

Page 748 *Asymetrical should read: Lacking symetry, not identical on both sides of a center line.*

Page 749 *Minaret should read: One or more balconies from which the muezzin calls...*

BIBLIOGRAPHY

Encyclopedia of British Pottery and Porcelain Marks. Geoffrey A. Godden. 1964.

Staffordshire Blue. W. L. Little. 1969.

Anglo-American China. Part 1 and Part 2. Sam Laidecker. 1954.

The Dictionary of Blue and White Printed Pottery 1780-1880. A. W. Coysh and R. K. Hemrywood. 1982.

English Transfer. Printed Pottery and Porcelain. Cye William-Wood. 1981.

British Pottery. Goeffrey A. Godden. 1975.

Sunderland Ware, The Potteries of Wearside. Sunderland Public Libraries, Museum and Art Gallery. 1973.

English Pottery and Porcelain. Paul Atterbury. 1978.

The Collector's Encyclopedia of English Ceramics. Bernard and Therle Hughes. 1968.

Scottish Pottery Historical Review No. 8, 1983/84.

For other references and further study please consult the Bibliography in Book I page 747.

Index of Patterns

F-Floral   G-Genre

C-Classic   J-Juvenile

O-Oriental   PC-Polychrome Chinoiserie

S-Scenic   M-Miscellaneous

*Pattern identified in Book I; description continued in the Supplement.

692

693

694

695

TYPESETTING BY VARICOMP INC.

PRINTING BY IMAGE PRINTING, INC.

LOUISVILLE, KENTUCKY